Building on The Rock
Facilitator's Edition

Preparing for Our Life Together

A Premarital Course for Couples

Acknowledgements

I would like to express my sincere thanks and well wishes to all the couples over the past 25 plus years who unknowingly contributed to this work. In a way you have seeded into generations of marriages yet to come!

A special word of gratitude goes to the pastors, biblical counselors, and ministry leaders who have dedicated themselves to walking alongside engaged couples on their journey toward marriage. Your faithfulness in guiding others toward a Christ-centered union is itself a gift to generations yet to come. It is my prayer that this resource will equip and encourage you as you pour into the lives of those entrusted to your care.

Building On The Rock
Facilitator's Edition

Preparing for Our Life Together

A Premarital Course for Couples

By

Dr. Gerard A. Ball DCCPsych

Oooan Biblical Publishing

A Division of Ocean Biblical Counseling, LLC

Building on the Rock A Biblical Premarital Course

A Letter to You the Facilitator!

What a joy it is to welcome you to this ministry!

The very fact that you are holding this guide in your hands says something wonderful about you - you have chosen to invest yourself in one of the most sacred and significant journeys a couple will ever take. The ancient wisdom of Scripture invites us to "study and show ourselves approved" (2 Timothy 2:15), and the couples entrusted to your care are doing exactly that. Your willingness to walk alongside them is itself a gift not only to them, but to the generations this couple will impact.

This course has been designed with one purpose in mind: to help engaged couples thoughtfully assess and strengthen their spiritual foundations as they prepare to enter into the Biblical covenant of marriage. As their Facilitator, you will be guiding them not just through questions of compatibility, but through God's beautiful design for what marriage can be at its very best. Let's face it, our Father invented marriage so Who else would know how to make it work?

As you prepare to lead couples through this material, here are a few things to keep in mind:

About the Format. This is an interactive workbook course. Each couple will have their own Student's Copy which they will work through individually and together. You will encounter two distinct types of sections throughout - Individual Reflection, where couples spend time with their own thoughts before God, and Couple Discussion, where they share and explore those reflections together. Both are equally valuable! Encourage couples to give each section their full attention. Encourage them to resist the temptation to skip ahead or over sections.

About Your Role. Each time you meet with a couple, they should bring their completed chapters with them. That meeting time is rich and intentional as your role is to walk through the material with them personally, listen carefully, ask thoughtful questions, and provide biblical guidance where needed. Their preparation will make all the difference, and so will yours.

About This Guide. This Facilitator's Copy contains everything in the Student's Copy along with additional teaching notes, discussion resources, and practical tools to help you lead the course as well as your personal evaluations after each meeting. Please address these with confidence and grace as you guide the conversations.

Before You Begin. The next few pages contain an introduction that will orient you to the material and the style of the workbook. Read it carefully and prayerfully before moving forward.

You are embarking on something truly meaningful. May God bless every conversation you facilitate, every couple you serve, and every step they take together on this road toward marriage. Know that your faithfulness to this ministry is building lives and legacies for His glory.

Are you ready? Now, let's begin!

Blessings,

Dr. Gerard (Gerry) Ball DCCP

Please turn to Facilitator's Introduction

right after the Table of Contents

and begin your journey toward

assisting your couple toward

a Christ-centered, Biblically

founded marriage

that will stand

the test of time!

Welcome

to

Building on the ROCK!

Table of Contents

A Letter from the Author v

Table of Contents viii

FACILITATOR'S GUIDE 1

Building on the Rock: A Biblical Foundation for Marriage 1

Introduction: Your Role as Pre-Marriage Facilitator 1

Philosophy and Approach 2

How to Use This Workbook 4

Chapter-by-Chapter Guidance 6

Handling Difficult Situations 15

Special Situations 17

Working with Different Couple Types 19

Self-Care for Advisors 20

Conclusion: Your Ministry Matters 21

Additional Resources for Advisors: 22

CHAPTER 1: YOUR FOUNDATION 23

CHAPTER 2: BUILDING ON BIBLICAL FOUNDATIONS 30

CHAPTER 3: SHARING YOUR PERSONAL HISTORY 43

CHAPTER 4: GOD'S DESIGN FOR MARRIAGE 60

CHAPTER 5: UNDERSTANDING EACH OTHER'S PERSONALITY 81

CHAPTER 6: GOD'S HEART FOR YOUR FINANCIAL WELL-BEING 98

CHAPTER 7: FAITHFUL STEWARDSHIP THROUGH TITHING 119

CHAPTER 8: GOD'S DESIGN FOR SEXUALITY IN MARRIAGE 143

APPENDICES 156

APPENDIX A: RECOMMENDED READING FOR COUPLES 156

APPENDIX B: RECOMMENDED READING FOR FACILITATORS 158

APPENDIX C: ASSESSMENT TOOLS & INVENTORIES 160

APPENDIX D: ONLINE RESOURCES & WEBSITES 162

APPENDIX E: HELPFUL FORMS & WORKSHEETS 164

APPENDIX F: WHEN TO REFER TO PROFESSIONAL COUNSELING 169

APPENDIX G: LEGAL REQUIREMENTS FOR MARRIAGE 170

APPENDIX H: SAMPLE WEDDING CEREMONY OUTLINE 171

APPENDIX I: POST-MARRIAGE FOLLOW-UP 173

ASSESSMENT FORMS 175

HOW TO USE THESE FORMS 175

FORM 1: INITIAL COUPLE INTAKE FORM 176

FORM 2: RELATIONSHIP HEALTH ASSESSMENT 180

RED FLAG ASSESSMENT 185

OVERALL READINESS ASSESSMENT 185

FORM 3: SESSION NOTES TEMPLATE 187

FORM 4: FINAL READINESS ASSESSMENT 190

FORM 5: COUPLE FEEDBACK FORM 193

FACILITATOR'S GUIDE

Building on the Rock: A Biblical Foundation for Marriage

Introduction: Your Role as Pre-Marriage Facilitator

Thank you for choosing to invest in the lives of your church's engaged couples. It is my opinion that marriage preparation is one of the most strategic ministries that one can invest in the church today. The reason is that the enemy is actively working to destroy marriage and the family and as you and I know marriage and family are the foundational building blocks of not only the church but also our society. By helping couples build a strong foundation before they exchange their vows, you are not merely preventing future challenges; you are strengthening their families for generations to come while advancing God's kingdom in powerful, lasting ways.

The work you are doing with marriage preparation will ripple through time. A couple well-prepared today will have a better foundation to become parents who model biblical marriage for their children tomorrow, and grandparents who will leave a legacy of faithfulness for decades to come. You are literally shaping the future of the church through your commitment to this ministry.

This section has been prepared as the Advisor's Guide and it has been designed to help you effectively mentor with the **Building on the Rock Premarital Workbook** for engaged couples. Whether you're a pastor, counselor, or mentor couple, this resource provides structure, guidance, and practical tips for leading couples through a series of comprehensive marriage preparation exercises designed to establish a solid biblical foundation for their lifelong covenant.

Thank you again, Dr. Gerry Ball

Philosophy and Approach

The Purpose of Pre-Marriage Guidance

Pre-marriage guidance serves several crucial purposes:

1. Assessment To evaluate whether this couple is ready for marriage. Not every engaged couple should proceed "to the altar." Your role includes discerning whether they have the spiritual maturity, relational health, emotional maturity and compatibility necessary to go forward with their marriage.

2. Education To teach biblical principles about various aspects of marriage that many couples have never even been exposed to. Most people enter engagement with incomplete views or inaccurate expectations of marriage usually shaped by culture, media, and dysfunctional examples they have witnessed rather than solid Scriptural teaching.

3. Preparation To help couples develop skills, establish healthy patterns, and create shared expectations before they exchange their vows. It's far easier to build correctly from here in the preparatory stage than for a counselor or pastor to attempt to repair a broken couple two, three or five years later.

4. Intervention To bring to the surface issues that may need addressing before they marry. Whether past wounds, theological differences, or concerning relational patterns, it's better to discover and address these during engagement than after the wedding.

5. Spiritual Foundation To help ensure that the couple builds their marriage on Christ and His Word rather than preconceived notions. Marriages built on romance, physical attraction, or shared interests alone will not withstand life's storms.

Key Principles for Facilitators

1. Create Safety Couples must feel safe to be honest. Establish confidentiality (with appropriate exceptions for abuse, criminal activity, etc.), avoid judgment, and create an environment where vulnerability is welcomed.

2. Ask, Don't Assume Don't assume you understand their backgrounds, beliefs, or situations. Ask questions, listen carefully, and seek to understand before offering advice.

3. Be Willing to Say, "Not Yet" This may be the hardest of all the principles you should consider. If a couple isn't ready for marriage, have the courage to recommend delaying the wedding. A postponed wedding is uncomfortable; a broken marriage is a disaster.

4. Focus on the Foundations This workbook emphasizes foundational issues - spiritual alignment, biblical roles, personality understanding, financial stewardship, etc. Keep couples focused on these essentials rather than getting sidetracked by secondary issues. The secondary issues will be there but stay focused.

5. Point to Scripture Your authority comes from God's Word, you're your personal opinion. Someone can always reject or debate a personal opinion, but not the Word of God. Always ground your good counsel in biblical truth, helping couples see that you're calling them to a standard set in place by the Holy Spirit, not your own preferences.

6. Pray Consistently Pray for each couple regularly. Pray before and during sessions. Invite the Holy Spirit to do what only He can do—convict, transform, and unite.

How to Use This Workbook

Recommended Timeline

Standard Timeline: 8-10 Sessions - Recommended

- **Session 1**: Introduction, Overview, Chapter 1 Discussion
- **Session 2**: Chapter 1 Review & Chapter 2 Discussion
- **Session 3**: Chapter 2 Review & Chapter 3 Discussion
- **Session 4**: Chapter 3 Review & Chapter 4 Discussion
- **Session 5**: Chapter 4 Review & Chapter 5 Disc Assessment
- **Session 6**: Chapter 5 Review & Chapter 6 Discussion
- **Session 7**: Chapter 6 Review & Chapter 7 Discussion
- **Session 8**: Chapter 7 Review & Chapter 8 Discussion
- **Session 9-10** Chapter 8 Review & Final Review
- (Optional): Additional topics as needed

Accelerated Timeline: 8 Sessions

If time is limited, you can sequence the chapters:

- Session 1: Introduction, Chapter 1
- Session 2: Chapter 2
- Session 3: Chapter 3
- Session 4: Chapter 4
- Session 5: Chapter 5 – Disc Assessment
- Session 6: Chapter 6
- Session 7: Chapter 7
- Session 8: Chapter 8

Extended Timeline: 12-16 Sessions

For couples with complex backgrounds or significant issues, extend the timeline:

- Spend 2 sessions on challenging chapters
- Add sessions on communication skills
- Include sessions on conflict resolution
- Address specific issues unique to the couple

Session Structure

Before Each Session:

- Review the couple's completed chapter work
- Note areas of concern, disagreement, or incomplete responses
- Pray for wisdom and discernment
- Prepare specific questions for discussion

During Each Session (60-90 minutes):

1. Opening (5-10 minutes)

- Welcome and prayer
- Check in: "How are you doing as a couple?"
- Briefly review what you'll cover today

2. Review Individual Work (15-20 minutes)

- Ask each person to share key insights from their individual reflections
- Note areas where they struggled or had questions
- Affirm honest, thoughtful responses

3. Discuss Couple Exercises (20-30 minutes)

- Review their couple discussion responses
- Explore areas of disagreement or confusion
- Ask probing questions to go deeper
- Address any red flags you've noticed

4. Teach and Apply (15-20 minutes)

- Reinforce key biblical principles from the chapter
- Share relevant examples or stories
- Provide additional context or teaching as needed
- Connect concepts to their specific situation

5. Assign Next Chapter (5 minutes)

- Walk through the next chapter briefly
- Highlight particularly important sections
- Set deadline for completion
- Answer any questions

6. Closing (5 minutes)

- Summarize key takeaways
- Pray together
- Encourage them in their preparation journey

After Each Session:

- Make notes about concerns, progress, and areas to revisit
- Pray for the couple
- Determine if any follow-up is needed before next session

Chapter-by-Chapter Guidance

Chapter 1: Your Spiritual Foundation Together

Key Goals:

- Confirm both parties are genuinely saved
- Assess spiritual maturity and growth trajectory
- Establish commitment to shared church life
- Identify any spiritual incompatibility

Red Flags to Watch For:

- One person is not a believer (unequally yoked - 2 Corinthians 6:14)
- Significant theological differences on <u>essential doctrines</u>
- One person is spiritually apathetic or stagnant
- No commitment to regular church involvement
- Different churches with no plan to unite in one

Discussion Questions to Add:

- "Tell me about your conversion experience in detail."
- "How has your faith affected your dating relationship?"
- "What does spiritual leadership look like to you?"
- "How do you handle spiritual differences or disagreements?"

When to Intervene: If one person is not saved, you must address this directly. A Christian should not marry an unbeliever. If there's a genuine question about salvation, (one is not born again, born of the spirit) help them understand the gospel and make a clear commitment before proceeding. At this point there is no going forward. You can opt to suggest they discuss salvation together and return at the next scheduled session so you can answer any questions or lead the person in a salvation prayer.

If they're attending different churches with no plan to unite, strongly urge them to make a decision during the engagement time. A divided Sunday morning creates long-term problems. Statistically, a two church family will become a no church family.

Chapter 2: Building on Biblical Foundations

Key Goals:

- Ensure understanding of whole created human being (spirit, soul, & body)
- Assess each person's spiritual health and Holy Spirit experience
- Identify spiritual gifts and ministry visions
- Discuss how spiritual health affects marriage

Red Flags to Watch For:

- Significant differences in understanding of Holy Spirit baptism that creates division
- One person spiritually mature, the other immature
- No awareness of spiritual gifts or ministry calling
- Neglect of physical or emotional health
- Unresolved emotional wounds affecting relationship

Discussion Questions to Add:

- "How do you see your emotional health affecting your relationship?"
- "What unhealed wounds might you bring into marriage?"
- "How will you support each other's spiritual growth practically?"
- "What happens when one of you is in a spiritual dry season?"

When to Intervene: If theological differences about the Holy Spirit are creating division or superiority, help them find unity on essentials while allowing freedom on secondary issues.

If significant emotional or mental health issues are present (depression, anxiety, trauma), recommend professional Christian counseling before proceeding with marriage.

Chapter 3: Sharing Your Personal History

Key Goals:

- Surface any past relationships, marriages, or children
- Assess healing from past wounds
- Understand family backgrounds and dynamics
- Identify potential extended family challenges

Red Flags to Watch For:

- Hidden past relationships or marriages
- Unresolved custody or child support issues
- Active co-parenting conflicts with ex-spouse
- Children who are strongly opposed to the marriage
- Toxic extended family dynamics without boundaries
- Significant secrets being revealed for first time
- Different approaches to stepparenting without resolution

Discussion Questions to Add:

- "How do your children feel about this marriage specifically?"
- "What contact do you have with your ex-spouse and how will you manage that?"
- "What family patterns do you want to continue/break in your marriage?"
- "How will you handle holidays when families compete for your time?"

When to Intervene: If past marriage wounds are clearly unhealed, recommend individual counseling before proceeding.

If children are strongly opposed or struggling, consider delaying the wedding and involving family counseling.

If extended family boundaries are non-existent and causing current problems, help the couple establish clear boundaries before marriage.

If significant secrets emerge during this chapter (hidden children, undisclosed debt, criminal history), address the breach of trust directly.

Chapter 4: God's Design for Marriage

Key Goals:

- Establish biblical understanding of covenant vs. contract
- Clarify roles: husband's calling to lead/love, wife's calling to respect/support
- Address any egalitarian/complementarian tensions
- Ensure both understand and accept the biblical design

Red Flags to Watch For:

- Fundamental disagreement about biblical roles
- Man expecting dominance rather than servant leadership
- Woman resistant to any form of submission
- Either person holding extreme/unbiblical views
- Cultural or family expectations overriding Scripture
- One person paying lip service but clearly not committed

Discussion Questions to Add:

- "What does spiritual leadership look like in daily life?"
- "How will you handle decisions when you disagree?"
- "What concerns do you have about your spouse's understanding of their role?"
- "How will you know if leadership becomes domination or submission becomes enabling?"

When to Intervene: If they have fundamental disagreement about biblical roles, don't proceed until resolved. This isn't a minor issue—it affects every aspect of marriage.

If the man shows signs of controlling behavior or the woman shows signs of manipulative behavior, address directly and consider requiring counseling.

Help them distinguish between biblical complementarianism (mutual respect with different roles) and cultural patriarchy (oppressive male dominance).

Chapter 5: Understanding Each Other's Personality

Key Goals:

- Complete personality assessment together
- Identify personality differences and complementarity
- Address "fixer" mentality
- Develop appreciation for differences

Red Flags to Watch For:

- One person trying to change the other constantly
- Extreme personality differences creating constant conflict
- Inability to appreciate differences
- One person's personality traits indicating potential problems (extreme narcissism, severe anxiety, etc.)
- Contempt for partner's personality

Discussion Questions to Add:

- "What frustrates you most about your partner's personality?"
- "How do you typically respond when annoyed by personality differences?"
- "What personality traits in your partner do you hope will change after marriage?"
- "How will you support each other during stressful times given your different styles?"

Suggested Assessment Tools:

- DISC Assessment - Recommended
- Myers-Briggs Type Indicator
- Enneagram
- StrengthsFinder
- Your church's preferred personality inventory

When to Intervene: If personality differences are creating significant current conflict in front of you, they'll create more conflict privately when married. Help them develop strategies now.

If one person shows signs of a personality disorder or severe mental health issues, recommend professional evaluation before proceeding.

Chapter 6: God's Heart for Your Financial Well-Being

Key Goals:

- Establish biblical theology of prosperity and provision
- Identify money mindsets and beliefs
- Address poverty mentality or prosperity gospel extremes
- Build faith in God as provider

Red Flags to Watch For:

- Extreme views (health/wealth/money gospel or poverty mentality)
- Fundamental disagreement about God's provision
- One person controlled by fear about money
- One person controlled by greed or materialism
- Unrealistic expectations about finances

Discussion Questions to Add:

- "What's your biggest fear about money in marriage?"
- "How did your parents handle finances and how has that shaped you?"
- "What does 'God as your source' mean practically?"
- "How will you handle it if you face significant financial hardship?"

When to Intervene: If they hold extreme or unbiblical views about prosperity, teach balanced biblical theology before proceeding.

This chapter sets up Chapter 7 (tithing), so ensure they understand foundational principles before moving to practical application.

Chapter 7: Faithful Stewardship Through Tithing

Key Goals:

- Establish commitment to tithing
- Determine where tithe will go
- Address objections and concerns
- Create practical giving plan

Red Flags to Watch For:

- Fundamental disagreement about tithing
- Unwillingness to tithe due to debt or expenses
- Planning to split tithe between multiple places
- One person committed to tithing, other resistant
- Attitude of entitlement or lack of gratitude

Discussion Questions to Add:

- "What specific obstacles make tithing difficult for you?"
- "How will you handle it if one person wants to tithe and the other doesn't?"
- "What will you do when money is extremely tight?"
- "Have you ever experienced God's provision through tithing?"

When to Intervene: If they disagree about tithing, help them work toward unity before marriage. This isn't just about money - it's about trust, obedience to God's Word, and setting priorities.

If they claim they "can't afford" to tithe, stop and work with them on their budget together. Often the issue is spending priorities, not actual inability.

If they're planning to split the tithe among multiple ministries, teach the storehouse principle clearly.

Chapter 8: God's Design for Sexuality in Marriage

Key Goals:

- Establish understanding of God's design for sexual intimacy
- Identify and address past wounds or unhealthy patterns
- Create a framework for healthy sexual relationships
- Establish protective boundaries before marriage
- Ensure both partners are entering marriage with sexual integrity

Red Flags to Watch For:

- Current sexual activity
- Active pornography use by either party
- Significant unresolved trauma or abuse history (Refer out for counseling)
- Vastly different expectations about frequency or practices
- Shame, fear, or disgust about sexuality

- One partner intimating that withholding or using sex as manipulation/control
- Unwillingness to discuss boundaries or establish accountability
- Gray area practices that violate mutuality, honor, or biblical boundaries
- Evidence of "out of bounds" expressions (past or present)
- Expectation that marriage will "fix" sexual sin patterns

Discussion Questions to Add:

- "How have past experiences (positive or negative) shaped your views about sexuality?"
- "Are there any areas of sexual sin you need to address before marriage?" (Remember, you are moving towards repentance)
- "Which of the Four Essentials (Mutuality, Oneness, Honor/Respect, No Shame) concerns you most?"
- "What specific boundaries will protect your marriage bed?"
- "How will you handle differences in desire or expectations?"
- "Do either of you carry wounds that need healing before marriage?"
- "What accountability structures will you put in place regarding technology/entertainment?"

When to Intervene:

If they're currently sexually active: Stop immediately and address this directly. This is a critical red flag indicating they're not honoring God's design even before marriage. They need accountability, repentance, and a plan for maintaining purity until the wedding. Do not proceed until this is resolved.

If pornography is involved: This must be addressed before marriage. Refer to resources (Surfing for God for men, similar resources for women). Establish accountability partners of the same gender. This pattern will not magically stop after marriage - it will worsen. (Refer for counseling)

If significant trauma exists: Refer for counseling immediately. Sexual abuse, assault, or significant dysfunction requires specialized help beyond premarital guidance. Do not minimize this or assume "love will heal it."

If expectations are vastly different: Help them have honest conversations about expectations, frequency, and practices. Silence now creates major problems later. Use the "gray area" questions to guide these discussions.

If one shows entitlement attitudes: Address immediately. Sex is not a right to be demanded but a gift to be shared mutually. Any hint of coercion, manipulation, or entitlement reveals dangerous patterns. Address.

If boundaries are unclear or weak: Do not let them enter marriage without clear, agreed-upon protections: no pornography, complete electronic device accountability, entertainment standards, how to handle attraction to others, etc.

Teaching Emphasis:

- The Four Elements (Physical, Emotional, Relational, Spiritual) work together—you can't isolate physical from the others
- The Four Essentials (Mutuality, Oneness, Honor/Respect, No Shame) are non-negotiable boundaries
- Marriage does not fix sexual sin—it reveals and often intensifies existing patterns
- Healing from past wounds is possible but requires intentional work
- God's design is protective, not restrictive; liberating, not limiting
- Sexual intimacy reflects Christ and the Church—it's sacred, not just physical

Critical Conversation: Before concluding this chapter, ask directly: "Is there anything in your sexual history - individually or as a couple - that needs to be addressed before marriage?" Give them space to answer honestly. Many couples will minimize or hide issues. Watch for evasiveness, defensiveness, or reluctance to make eye contact.

If either admits to current sexual sin, pornography use, or past trauma, do not rush past it. These issues require focused attention and possibly professional referral before proceeding with marriage preparation.

Note to Advisors: This is often the most uncomfortable chapter for both couples and advisors, but it's critically important. Many marriages struggle or fail because sexual issues were never addressed before the wedding. Your willingness to ask hard questions and create space for honest conversation may save their marriage from years of pain.

Don't assume Christian couples are maintaining purity - statistics show many are not. Don't assume past abuse won't affect the marriage - it almost always does without healing. Don't assume they understand God's design - most have been discipled more by culture than Scripture in this area.

Be pastoral in form, be direct, be compassionate, and be willing to delay the wedding if significant issues emerge that require more time to address.

Handling Difficult Situations

When You Discover Major Issues

Red Flag Categories:

STOP Flags - Recommend Delaying/Canceling Wedding:

- One person is not a believer
- Active addiction (substance abuse, pornography, gambling)
- Evidence of abuse (physical, emotional, spiritual)
- Unresolved legal issues (active warrants, pending charges, divorce not finalized)
- Significant mental health crisis requiring immediate treatment
- Pattern of deception or major lies discovered
- Adultery during engagement
- Fundamental incompatibility on essential issues

CAUTION Flags - Require Additional Counseling:

- Past abuse (victim or perpetrator) without professional counseling
- Significant debt without plan or hidden from partner
- Unresolved trauma affecting relationship
- Premarital sexual activity without repentance
- Blended family issues needing specialized help
- Extended family dysfunction requiring boundaries
- One person significantly pressured into marriage

ATTENTION Flags - Monitor and Address:

- Conflict resolution skills need development
- Communication patterns need improvement
- Different expectations about roles, parenting, etc.
- Some financial irresponsibility
- Moderate family dysfunction
- Personality differences creating friction

How to Recommend Delaying a Wedding

This is one of the most difficult conversations you'll have, but sometimes necessary. Here's how to approach it:

1. Schedule a Serious Meeting Don't drop this casually. Schedule dedicated time and let them know you have serious concerns to discuss.

2. Be Direct but Compassionate "I care about you both deeply, which is why I need to share some concerns. Based on what I've observed through our sessions, I believe you should consider delaying your wedding. Here's why..."

3. Be Specific Don't make vague statements. Identify specific issues: "The pattern of conflict I've seen where you [specific behavior] and she [specific response] is concerning because..."

4. Offer a Path Forward Don't just say "don't get married." Offer a plan: "I recommend you delay the wedding for at least six months while you work with a counselor on [specific issues]. If you make progress in these areas, we can reassess."

5. Acknowledge the Cost "I know this is painful. I know you've made plans, told people, invested money. But I'd rather you be disappointed now than divorced later."

6. Point to Scripture and Their Good "Proverbs says 'Faithful are the wounds of a friend.' I'm speaking truth because I love you and want God's best for your marriage. This recommendation comes from concern, not judgment."

7. Leave the Decision with Them "Ultimately, this is your choice. I can't force you to delay. But I'm telling you my strong good counsel as someone who cares about you and has walked this path with many couples."

8. Establish Boundaries "If you choose to proceed despite my counsel, I won't be able to perform the ceremony. But I'll remain available to continue working with you if you decide to delay and address these issues."

When Couples Disagree with Your Assessment

Some couples will resist your counsel. They may:

- Minimize the issues you've identified
- Blame you for being too strict or traditional
- Accuse you of trying to break them up
- Proceed with the wedding despite your counsel

Your Response:

- Remain calm and compassionate
- Reiterate your concerns clearly
- Document your counsel in writing (You should be documenting everything anyway)
- Maintain your boundaries (don't perform ceremony if you believe they shouldn't marry or in the case the officiant needs you to sign off on the wedding)
- Continue praying for them – I mean "really praying for them".
- Remain available if they later recognize the wisdom of your counsel

Remember: Your job is to give good faithful direction, not to control their choices. Some couples will disregard wise advice and proceed anyway. Pray for them, but don't compromise your integrity by endorsing a marriage you believe is unwise.

Special Situations

Second Marriages

Additional Considerations:

- Ensure divorce was biblical and any period of restoration has been completed
- Assess healing from previous marriage
- Address complications: children, ex-spouses, financial obligations
- Discuss how previous marriage/s can influence this one
- Ensure they're not repeating patterns

Questions to Add:

- "What role did you play in the breakdown of your previous marriage?"
- "How has God healed you from that experience?" (Repentance?)
- "What are you doing differently this time?"
- "How will you handle contact with your ex-spouse?"

Significant Age Differences

Additional Considerations:

- Assess maturity levels (are they in similar life stages?)
- Discuss implications: childbearing years, retirement timing, health, life expectancy
- Watch for power imbalance or unhealthy dynamics
- Ensure families are supportive

Cohabitation Before Marriage

Your Response:

- Address biblically without shame or condemnation
- Call to repentance and commitment to purity until wedding
- Discuss living separately until marriage – let them work it out
- Acknowledge this makes marriage preparation more challenging (they're already functioning as married)
- Don't perform wedding if they refuse to live separately

Cross-Cultural or Interfaith Marriages

Additional Considerations:

- If interfaith (Christian marrying non-Christian), strongly counsel against (2 Corinthians 6:14)
- If cross-cultural (both Christian), discuss how cultural differences affect expectations about roles, family, finances, etc.
- Help them navigate family opposition if present
- Ensure they're not ignoring significant cultural barriers

Working with Different Couple Types

The Eager Couple

Characteristics:

- Completes all work thoroughly and on time
- Engages deeply in discussions
- Asks thoughtful questions
- Shows spiritual maturity

Your Approach:

- Affirm their diligence
- Go deeper on topics
- Challenge them to think ahead to challenges they haven't anticipated
- Equip them to mentor other couples eventually

The Reluctant Couple

Characteristics:

- Completes work minimally or late
- Gives surface-level answers
- Views counseling as hoop to jump through
- Resistant to topics they find uncomfortable

Your Approach:

- Address the resistance directly: "I'm sensing some hesitation. What's going on?"
- Explain the why behind the work: "This isn't busy work. Here's why this matters..."
- Create accountability with deadlines
- Consider whether resistance indicates deeper issues

The Conflicted Couple

Characteristics:

- Frequent arguments during sessions
- Significant disagreements on multiple topics
- Tension visible in body language

- One or both defensive

Your Approach:

- Address the conflict: "I notice tension between you. Let's talk about it."
- Teach conflict resolution skills
- Help them communicate effectively
- Assess whether they're ready for marriage or need more time/counseling

The Imbalanced Couple

Characteristics:

- One person significantly more mature, engaged, or articulate
- One dominates conversation
- One defers completely to the other
- Power imbalance evident

Your Approach:

- Draw out the quieter person: "I'd like to hear from you specifically."
- Gently quiet the dominant person: "Let's hear from your partner now."
- Watch for concerning patterns (control, intimidation, excessive passivity)
- Address imbalance directly if unhealthy

Self-Care for Advisors

Marriage guidance is emotionally demanding work. To serve couples effectively long-term:

1. Maintain Your Own Marriage You can't give what you don't have. Invest in your own marriage continuously.

2. Set Boundaries

- Limit how many couples you guide simultaneously
- Don't schedule at all hours – set your hours of availability and stick to them
- Maintain appropriate emotional boundaries
- Refer couples to counselors when needed

3. Process Difficult Cases

- Debrief with oversight pastor, a trusted pastor or counselor
- Pray through heavy situations
- Don't carry the weight of couples' choices

4. Celebrate Successes

- Acknowledge when couples grow and thrive
- Attend weddings when possible
- Stay connected with couples post-marriage
- Let success stories encourage you

5. Know When to Refer You're not equipped to handle every situation. Refer to professional Christian counselors when couples need:

- Trauma recovery
- Addiction treatment
- Mental health intervention
- Complex family systems work
- Intensive therapy

Conclusion: Your Ministry Matters

Thank you for taking seriously the responsibility of marriage preparation. The work you're doing has eternal significance. Strong marriages create stable families, raise godly children, and display the gospel to watching world.

Not every couple you engage will have a successful marriage. Some will disregard your wisdom. Some will divorce despite your best efforts. But many will build strong, Christ-centered marriages because you invested in their foundation.

Years from now, you'll see couples you guided serving together in ministry, raising children who love Jesus, and mentoring younger couples. You'll know that your investment in their pre-marriage preparation bore lasting fruit.

Stay faithful. Speak truth in love. Point couples to Christ and His Word. Trust the Holy Spirit to do what only He can do. And know that your labor in the Lord is not in vain.

Additional Resources for Advisors:

Please see Resources in the Appendices

The Resources contained in the Appendices are tools to enhance your marriage preparation ministry. You will not need every resource listed so choose what fits your context, theology, and the specific needs of couples you serve. You may copy and distribute any and all of these Resources at will. It is my prayer that they will be useful in blessing and enriching both you and your couples.

The most important resources you bring are your own faithfulness to God's Word, your commitment to speak truth in love, and your willingness to invest in your couples' lives. Let these materials serve that calling, not replace it.

Remember: You're not just preparing couples for a wedding day. You're equipping them for a lifetime covenant that will display God's glory for decades to come. This eternal perspective makes all the difference.

May God bless your ministry to engaged couples, and may the marriages you help prepare be strong, Christ-centered, and fruitful for His kingdom.

Questions or Support:

Dr. Gerry Ball – gerry@oceanbiblicalcounseling.com

CHAPTER 1: YOUR FOUNDATION

Introduction: Building on the Rock

Jesus concluded His Sermon on the Mount with a powerful illustration about two builders - one who built his house on rock and another who built on sand. When the storms came, only the house built on rock remained standing (Matthew 7:24-27). As you prepare for marriage, you're not just planning a wedding; you're building a life together. The foundation you establish now will determine how well your marriage weathers the inevitable storms of life.

This chapter will help you examine and strengthen your God centered foundation as a couple. You'll explore your individual faith journeys, discuss your church involvement, and create a shared vision for spiritual growth in your marriage. Remember, a marriage built on a shared commitment to Christ has access to divine wisdom, supernatural strength, and eternal purpose that transcends the natural challenges of married life.

Part A: Understanding Salvation

Teaching: Why Salvation Matters in Marriage

Before we can discuss growing together spiritually, we need to establish that you're both actually on the same spiritual journey. Salvation - the act of placing your faith in Jesus Christ for forgiveness of sins and eternal life - is not just "fire insurance" or a ticket to heaven. It's the beginning of a transformational relationship with God that affects every area of your life, including your marriage.

What the Bible Says About Salvation:

Salvation is a gift from God, not something we earn through good works. Ephesians 2:8-9 tells us, *"For it is by grace you have been saved, through faith - and this is not from yourselves, it is the gift of God - not by works, so that no one can boast."* When we acknowledge our sin, believe that Jesus died on the cross for our sins and rose from the dead, when we surrender our lives to Him as Lord, we become "born again" (John 3:3) and we become new creations (2 Corinthians 5:17).

Why This Matters for Your Marriage:

When both partners are genuinely saved, you share:

- **The same ultimate authority** (God's Word guides your decisions)
- **The same value system** (biblical principles shape your priorities)
- **The same power source** (the Holy Spirit empowers you to love each other sacrificially)
- **The same eternal perspective** (you're building something that lasts beyond this now)
- **Access to spiritual disciplines together** (prayer, worship, Bible studies)

If one partner is saved and the other is not, you're operating from fundamentally different worldviews. The Bible calls this being "unequally yoked" (2 Corinthians 6:14), which creates friction and limits intimacy both spiritually and emotionally. If you're uncertain about your salvation or your partner's, this is the most important conversation you'll have during your engagement. Why not begin that conversation right now!

Individual Reflection (Each person completes separately first):

1. In your own words, what does it mean to be saved?

Consider: Do you understand salvation as a personal relationship with Jesus, or merely as religious activity? Can you articulate the gospel - that we're all sinners, Jesus died in our place, and we must personally receive Him and His atoning work by faith?

2. When did you make the decision to follow Christ? Describe that experience.

Consider: Was there a specific moment of conversion, or did you grow up in the church? Either way, when did your faith become personal rather than inherited? What were the circumstances? What changed in your life afterward?

3. How has your relationship with God grown since then?

Consider: Is your faith deeper now than it was a year ago? Five years ago? What spiritual disciplines (prayer, Bible reading, worship, fellowship) characterize your current walk with God? Have you experienced seasons of spiritual dryness or doubt? How did you navigate them?

---

4. What role do you want faith to play in your marriage?

Consider: Do you see faith as the center of your marriage, or as one compartment among many? How do you envision prayer, Bible study, church involvement, and spiritual leadership functioning in your home? What does a "Christ-centered marriage" look like to you practically?

Couple Discussion Questions:

1. Share your salvation testimonies with each other.

Take turns sharing your full story without interruption. Listen carefully to each other, ask clarifying questions, and celebrate what God has done in each of your lives. If either of you has uncertainty about your salvation, discuss this openly and consider meeting with your pastor or a mature believer.

---

2. How are your faith journeys similar? Different?

Identify commonalities (similar backgrounds, conversion experiences, or spiritual growth patterns) and differences (denominational traditions, theological emphases, or spiritual temperament). Differences aren't necessarily problems - they can enrich your marriage - but they need to be understood and navigated with grace.

---

3. What excites you most about growing spiritually together?

Dream together about what your spiritual life as a couple could look like. Share specific hopes: praying together daily, serving in ministry together, raising children in the faith, or encouraging each other's spiritual growth.

Part B: Your Church Life—Past, Present, and Future

Teaching: The Church's Role in Your Marriage

The church is not optional for Christians. Hebrews 10:24-25 commands us: *"And let us consider how we may spur one another on toward love and good deeds, not giving up meeting together, as some are in the habit of doing, but encouraging one another - and all the more as you see the Day approaching."*

Why Church Matters for Married Couples:

1. Accountability and Community Marriage is difficult, and you'll need the support, wisdom, and accountability of the leadership and other mature believers. The church offers a spiritual family that can pray for you, counsel you, and walk alongside you through daily challenges.

2. Corporate Worship While personal devotions are important, corporate worship offers something unique - joining with other believers to glorify God, hear His Word taught/preached, and participating in the ordinances of Baptism and Communion. These shared experiences will strengthen your faith and remind you that you're part of something bigger than yourselves.

3. Spiritual Leadership and Teaching A healthy body of believers provides biblically sound teaching that will help shape your marriage. You'll learn about biblical manhood and womanhood, the roles of husband and wife, conflict resolution, parenting (eventually), financial stewardship, and countless other practical life lessons based on the Word of God.

4. Service Opportunities God has gifted both of you for service in His kingdom (1 Peter 4:10). The church is the primary context where those gifts are developed and deployed. Serving together - whether in children's ministry, hospitality, service ministries, or outreach - strengthens your partnership and keeps you focused outward rather than becoming self-absorbed.

5. Intergenerational Relationships The church connects you with believers of all ages. Older couples can mentor you in marriage, while younger believers benefit from your example. This intergenerational community provides wisdom, perspective, and continuity.

Assessment for Each Person:

1. Current church attendance: How often? How long at this church?

Be honest about your attendance patterns. Sporadic attendance often signals that church hasn't become a true priority. If you've recently started attending more regularly, what changed? If you've been at your church for years, what has kept you there?

---

2. What do you value most about corporate worship?

Consider: The preaching? The music? The community? The liturgy? The sense of God's presence? The sacraments? Understanding what you value helps identify what you're looking for in a church as a married couple.

---

3. Are you currently serving in ministry? If so, describe your role.

Include formal roles (teaching, serving on the worship team) and informal service (hospitality, helps, etc.). How much time does this require? What do you enjoy about it? What challenges does it present?

---

4. If not serving, what's holding you back?

Common barriers include: uncertainty about your gifts, perceived time constraints, fear of commitment, past negative experiences, feeling unqualified, or simply never being asked. Identifying the barrier is the first step to overcoming it.

---

5. What would be one positive thing you can do now to take a step towards serving in ministry?

This should be specific and actionable: "Talk to the children's ministry director about opportunities," "Attend the volunteer orientation," "Pray about where God wants me to serve," or "Complete the spiritual gifts assessment our church offers."

Future Planning Together:

1. What kind of church do you want to attend as a married couple?

Discuss denominational preferences, worship style, church size, theological emphases, and practical considerations like location and service times. Be honest about non-negotiables versus preferences. For example: "I must have expositional preaching" (non-negotiable) versus "I prefer contemporary worship music" (preference).

---

2. How important is it that you attend the same church?

Married couples should worship together at the same church. Attending different churches divides your spiritual community, complicates your schedule, and can create competing loyalties. The Bible says that "the two have become one flesh…" Attending two different churches works against that oneness. What would it take for one of you to visit/join the other's church? Are you willing to explore new churches together? How will you make this decision?

---

3. What ministries or service opportunities interest you both?

Look for areas of overlap in your gifts and passions. Maybe you both love working with youth, have a heart for the poor, or enjoy creative projects. Serving together strengthens your bond and gives you shared purpose beyond yourselves. Also identify individual ministry interests - you don't have to do everything together.

---

4. How will you handle it if you have different preferences about church involvement?

What if one of you wants to attend every church event while the other prefers minimal involvement? What if one person's ministry commitment requires significant time away from home? Discuss how you'll balance individual ministry callings with your responsibility to prioritize your marriage and (eventually) family.

Action Steps:

1. Visit each other's churches if you attend different ones

Attend at least one full Sunday (worship service and ideally a Bible class or small group) at each church. Approach with openness rather than criticism. What could you appreciate about this church? Could you see yourself worshiping here? Take notes and discuss your impressions afterward.

---

2. Identify one ministry opportunity you could explore together

Before your wedding, commit to exploring at least one avenue of service together. This could be as simple as volunteering for a church workday, helping with a special event, or joining a short-term mission's team, Greeter, Usher, etc. The goal is to experience the joy of serving alongside each other.

Closing Reflection: Your Covenant Before God

As you complete this chapter, remember that a Christian marriage is more than a contract between two people, it's a covenant made before and with God. Your spiritual foundation isn't just for your benefit; it's so your marriage can be a testimony to God's faithfulness and love. When your marriage reflects Christ's love for the church (Ephesians 5:25-32), it becomes a powerful witness to a watching world.

Take time to pray together, perhaps for the first time as an engaged couple. Thank God for bringing you together, ask Him to strengthen your faith, and commit to building your marriage on the solid rock of His Word.

Prayer Suggestion:

"Father, thank You for the gift of salvation and for bringing us together. We want to build our marriage on the foundation of Christ. Help us to grow in our faith individually and together. Guide us to a church where we can worship, serve, and be equipped for Your purposes. Give us unity in spiritual matters and patience with each other as we grow. May our marriage bring glory to Your name. In Jesus' name, Amen."

CHAPTER 2: BUILDING ON BIBLICAL FOUNDATIONS

Introduction: Knowing Yourself to Love Your Spouse

One of the most profound statements in Scripture about marriage comes from Ephesians 5:28-29: "*Husbands ought to love their own wives as their own bodies; he who loves his wife loves himself. For no one ever hated his own flesh, but nourishes and cherishes it.*" This passage reveals an important truth: you cannot properly love your spouse if you don't understand yourself.

But what does it mean to truly understand yourself? Modern psychology offers insights about personality, attachment styles, and behavioral patterns - all valuable tools. However, the Bible provides a deeper framework: you are a tripartite being created in God's image, and are composed of spirit, soul, and body. Understanding this biblical anthropology (the study of human nature) will help you grasp how you function, where you need growth, and how to build a marriage that honors God in every dimension of your being.

This chapter will explore the three-part nature of humanity and examine how the Holy Spirit works in your life to transform you into the image of Christ. As you grow in self-awareness and spiritual maturity, you'll be better equipped to love your future spouse with wisdom, patience, and Christ-like sacrifice.

Part A: Understanding Your Whole Person - Spirit, Soul, and Body

Teaching: The Tripartite Nature of Humanity

Learning Together: Read 1 Thessalonians 5:23

"Now may the God of peace Himself sanctify you completely; and may your whole spirit, soul, and body be preserved blameless at the coming of our Lord Jesus Christ."

This verse reveals that human beings are not simple, one-dimensional creatures. We are complex beings with three distinct yet interconnected parts: spirit, soul, and body. Understanding these three dimensions helps us comprehend how sin affects us, how salvation transforms us, and how we can grow toward wholeness in Christ.

Why This Matters for Marriage:

Marriage is a comprehensive union – a covenant relationship. Genesis 2:24 says a husband and wife become "one flesh," but this oneness extends beyond physical intimacy. In a healthy Christian marriage, couples experience:

- **Spiritual unity** (praying together, worshiping together, growing in faith together)
- **Soulish unity** (emotional intimacy, intellectual connection, aligned values)
- **Physical unity** (sexual intimacy, physical affection, caring for each other's health)

Problems in marriage often occur when we neglect one of these dimensions. A couple might have great physical chemistry but lack spiritual depth. Another couple might be spiritually aligned but struggle with emotional intimacy. Understanding the spirit-soul-body framework helps you identify where you're strong and where you need growth.

The Human Spirit: Your Connection to God

What Scripture Teaches About the Human Spirit:

One was of describing the spirit is to say that the spirit is the eternal part of us that is designed for communion with God. When God created Adam, He *"breathed into his nostrils the breath of life; and man became a living being"* (Genesis 2:7). This divine breath gave Adam a spirit that distinguished him from the animals and enabled him among other things to know God personally.

When man sinned and because of the law "like begets like" every person enters the world separated from God for God has declared his spirit dead. Dead in trespasses and sins (Ephesians 2:1) and eternally separated from God. This doesn't mean the spirit ceases to exist, but rather that it's separated from God and incapable of responding to spiritual truths. Romans 8:7 explains: *"The carnal mind is enmity against God; for it is not subject to the law of God, nor indeed can be."* An unregenerate spirit cannot please God or truly understand spiritual things (1 Corinthians 2:14).

The New Birth:

When you place your faith in Jesus the Christ, something supernaturally wonderful occurs - you are "*born again*" or "*born of the Spirit*" (John 3:3-8). God's Holy Spirit regenerates your human spirit, bringing it to life and uniting it with God. You become a "*new creation*" (2 Corinthians 5:17) with a transformed spirit that can now commune with God, discern spiritual truth, and produce spiritual fruit.

This regenerated spirit becomes the "command center" for the Christian life. Your spirit, now indwelt by the Holy Spirit, is meant to govern your soul (thoughts, emotions, will) and your body. When you're living according to the spirit rather than the flesh, you experience peace, joy, and spiritual vitality (Romans 8:5-6) and a relationship with the Father through the Son.

In Marriage:

When two people with regenerated spirits unite in marriage, they have the capacity for profound spiritual intimacy. You can pray together knowing God hears you both. You can encourage each other with spiritual truths. You can discern God's will together. However, this spiritual unity doesn't happen automatically - it must be cultivated through intentionality in the things of God and a shared commitment to grow in Christ.

Individual Study: The Human Spirit

1. What does Scripture teach about the human spirit?

Beyond what's already discussed, research these passages: Proverbs 20:27 (the spirit as a lamp), Romans 8:16 (the Spirit bearing witness with our spirit), 1 Corinthians 2:11 (the Spirit knowing our thoughts). What insights do you gain about the function and importance of the human spirit?

---

2. How does your spirit connect you to God?

Consider your personal experience: When do you feel most spiritually alive? What spiritual disciplines (prayer, worship, Scripture reading, fasting) strengthen your awareness of God's presence in your life? How does your spirit communicate with God – through His Word, impressions, convictions, peace, and the Holy Spirit?

---

3. What does it mean to be "born of the Spirit"? (John 3:3-8)

Read Jesus' conversation with Nicodemus carefully. Why is spiritual birth necessary? How is it different from physical birth? What does it mean that we cannot see or control the Spirit's work like the wind? How does this inform your understanding of salvation and sanctification?

The Soul: Your Mind, Will, and Emotions

Understanding the Soul:

The soul represents your personality, consciousness, and psychological makeup. While theologians debate the precise relationship between soul and spirit, Scripture distinguishes between them (Hebrews 4:12: "dividing soul and spirit"). For our discussions here, we can understand the soul as comprising three primary faculties:

1. The Mind (Your Intellect and Thought Life)

Your mind is where you process information, form beliefs, make judgments, and develop worldviews. Romans 12:2 calls for the "renewing of your mind," indicating that salvation doesn't automatically transform your thinking patterns. You must actively cooperate with the Holy Spirit to replace this world's lies with God's truths and to think according to God's Word.

In marriage, your mind affects how you interpret your spouse's words and actions, how you solve problems together, and whether you think biblically about roles, communications, and conflicts.

2. The Will (Your Capacity for Choice and Decision-Making)

Your will is your ability to make choices. While salvation transforms your spirit, your will remains active - you must daily choose to follow Christ rather than your sinful inclinations (Luke 9:23). Your will determines whether you'll obey God's Word, love sacrificially, forgive offenses, and pursue holiness.

In marriage, your will determines whether you'll keep your covenant vows when feelings fade, whether you'll serve your spouse when it's inconvenient, and whether you'll choose unity over being right to name a few.

3. The Emotions (Your Feelings and Affections)

Your emotions are God-given capacities to experience life richly - joy, sorrow, anger, love, fear, compassion, and countless other feelings. We were created as emotional beings. Emotions are not sinful in themselves (Jesus experienced the full range of human emotions), but they can lead us into sin when they're not submitted to God's truth and governed by the Holy Spirit.

In marriage, emotions provide color, intimacy, and connection. However, emotions can also deceive us (Jeremiah 17:9). Learning to acknowledge your emotions while not being controlled by them is crucial for marital health.

The Soul's Need for Transformation:

While your spirit is made new at salvation, your soul undergoes gradual transformation throughout your Christian life - a process called sanctification. Philippians 2:12-13 captures this dynamic: "*Work out your own salvation with fear and trembling; for it is God who works in you both to will and to do for His good pleasure.*" God works in you, but you must cooperate with that work.

When the Soul is Disconnected from the Father:

When you're not walking in intimate fellowship with God - through sin, neglect, or distraction - your soul is ruling you. You may experience:

- Mental confusion, anxiety, or obsessive thought patterns
- Emotional instability, depression, or numbness
- Weakened willpower, giving in to temptation more easily
- A sense of emptiness or purposelessness

In marriage, a dominating soul leads to unhealthy relationships. You project your unhealed wounds onto your spouse, make decisions based on fear rather than faith, become dominated by the "self", and struggle to love well. This is why being led by the spirit is essential for marital health.

Individual Study: The Soul

1. How do you see your mind, emotions, and will working in your daily life?

Reflect on a recent challenging situation. What thoughts went through your mind? What emotions did you experience? What choices did you make? How did these three aspects of your soul interact? Were they in harmony or conflict?

---

2. What areas of your soul need God's transformation?

Be specific and honest. Do you struggle with anxious thoughts? Uncontrolled anger? Emotional wounds from the past? Weak willpower in certain areas? Pride or insecurity? Identifying these areas is the first step toward inviting God's healing and transformation power.

---

3. How does disconnection from the Father affect the soul?

Recall a season when you were spiritually distant from God. How did it impact your mental state? Your emotional health? Your ability to make good decisions? What brought you back into close fellowship with God?

The Body: Your Physical Dwelling Place

The Body in Biblical Perspective:

Christianity holds a unique view of the body. Unlike Greek philosophy which saw the body as a prison for the soul, or materialism which sees the body as all we are, Christianity teaches that the body is a good gift from God that will be resurrected in glorified form (1 Corinthians 15:42-44).

The Body as God's Temple:

Scripture teaches us that the body takes on an even greater significance: *"Do you not know that your body is the temple of the Holy Spirit who is in you, whom you have from God, and you are not your own? For you were bought at a price;*

therefore, glorify God in your body and in your spirit, which are God's" (1 Corinthians 6:19-20).

This means your body is not merely your own possession to do with as you please. It belongs to God, and you are called to steward it well by:

- Maintaining physical health through proper nutrition, exercise, and rest
- Avoiding harmful substances that damage the body
- Practicing sexual purity, reserving sexual intimacy for marriage
- Using your body to serve God and others

The Body-Soul-Spirit Connection:

Your body, soul, and spirit are interconnected. Physical exhaustion affects your emotions and can affect your spiritual vitality. Chronic stress impacts your physical health. Spiritual disciplines like fasting affect both body and soul. You cannot compartmentalize these dimensions—they interconnected as part of the unified whole.

In Marriage:

Physical health and care directly impact your marriage. Sexual intimacy is a gift from God meant to unite husband and wife (1 Corinthians 7:3-5). Physical affection communicates love and builds connection. Caring for your body demonstrates love for your spouse - you're maintaining the person they'll spend their life with. Neglecting physical health burdens your spouse and limits your ability to serve them well.

Individual Study: The Body

1. How does God want you to honor Him with your physical body?

Consider: Are there areas where you've neglected your physical health? Do you struggle with food, exercise, sleep, or other physical disciplines? How can you better steward your body as God's temple? What specific changes might God be calling you to make?

---

2. What role does physical health play in spiritual well-being?

Reflect on times when physical illness, exhaustion, or neglect affected your spiritual life. How does your body's condition influence your ability to pray, serve, or worship? How might improving your physical health enhance your spiritual effectiveness?

Couple Discussion Questions:

1. How can understanding spirit, soul, and body strengthen our future marriage?

Discuss how understanding this tripartite framework can help you understand each other better. Talk about which dimension is currently ruling in your life. How can this understanding help you identify and address problems in your marriage more effectively?

---

2. In what ways can we help each other grow spiritually?

Be specific: Will you pray together daily? Study Scripture together? Attend church and small groups together? How will you encourage each other when one is spiritually struggling? What does spiritual leadership and partnership look like for you?

Part B: The Holy Spirit's Work in Your Lives

Teaching: The Person and Power of the Holy Spirit

The Holy Spirit is perhaps the most misunderstood member of the Triune Godhead. Some Christians virtually ignore Him, treating Him as an impersonal force rather than a divine Person. Others emphasize experiences with the Spirit but lack biblical understanding. For your marriage to flourish spiritually, you need a solid, biblical understanding of who the Holy Spirit is and how He works.

Who is the Holy Spirit?

The Holy Spirit is not an "it" but a "He" - the third Person of the Trinity, fully God, co-equal with the Father and the Son. Jesus called Him "the Helper" or

"Comforter" (John 14:16, 26) who would come after Jesus' ascension to dwell within believers. The Holy Spirit:

- Convicts of sin, righteousness, and judgment (John 16:8)
- Guides us into all truth (John 16:13)
- Empowers us for service (Acts 1:8)
- Produces spiritual fruit in our lives (Galatians 5:22-23)
- Distributes spiritual gifts for building up the church (1 Corinthians 12:7-11)
- Helps us pray (Romans 8:26)
- Confirms our identity as God's children (Romans 8:16)

The Baptism of the Holy Spirit:

Subsequent Baptism Experience Christians, particularly in Pentecostal and Charismatic traditions, distinguish between receiving the Holy Spirit at conversion and being baptized in the Holy Spirit as a subsequent, empowering experience. They point to Acts 2 (Pentecost), Acts 8 (Samaritans who believed but received the Spirit later), and Acts 19 (disciples in Ephesus) as examples of Spirit baptism occurring after conversion. This view often associates the Baptism of the Holy Spirit with speaking in tongues as initial evidence (Acts 2:4, 10:44-46, 19:6).

Finding Unity in Differences:

- Every believer receives the Holy Spirit at salvation (Romans 8:9)
- We need continuous filling and empowerment by the Spirit (Ephesians 5:18)
- The Spirit distributes gifts to believers for ministry (1 Corinthians 12)
- We should earnestly desire spiritual gifts, especially prophecy (1 Corinthians 14:1)
- The fruit of the Spirit matters more than spectacular gifts (1 Corinthians 13, Galatians 5:22-23)

Spiritual Gifts:

The Holy Spirit distributes gifts to every believer "as He wills" (1 Corinthians 12:11). These gifts are not natural talents or earned abilities - they are supernatural abilities for serving the body of Christ and advancing God's kingdom.

Scripture mentions various gifts, including:

- Speaking gifts: prophecy, teaching, words of wisdom and knowledge, tongues, interpretation of tongues
- Serving gifts: service/helps, giving, mercy, hospitality, administration
- Signifying gifts: healing, miracles, faith, discernment of spirits

Why Gifts Matter in Marriage:

Understanding your spiritual gifts helps you:

- Discover where God wants you to serve in the church
- Identify how you can minister together as a couple
- Appreciate how your gifts complement your spouse's gifts
- Avoid comparison or competition (Romans 12:3-8)
- Build up the body of Christ more effectively

The Holy Spirit in Decision-Making:

One of the most practical aspects of Spirit-filled living is how the Holy Spirit guides believers. He doesn't bypass your mind but works through Scripture, godly counsel, circumstances, and an inner witness of peace. In marriage, learning to seek the Spirit's guidance together in major decisions (career changes, financial choices, parenting decisions, ministry commitments) is crucial for staying aligned with God's plans for your lives individually and together.

Individual Reflection:

1. What is your understanding of the Baptism of the Holy Spirit?

Write out your current understanding based on Scripture, teaching you've received, and your church's position. Be honest about questions or uncertainties you have. This is a topic for exploration, not division.

2. Have you experienced this baptism? Describe your experience or your questions about it.

If you've had a definite experience you would call Spirit baptism, describe it: When did it happen? What led to it? How did it affect you? If you haven't or aren't sure, what questions do you have? What desires do you have for more of the Spirit's power in your life?

---

3. What spiritual gifts do you believe God has given you?

You may not be certain yet - that's okay. Based on what you've learned, what gifts do you think you might have? What have other mature Christians observed in you? What ministry activities bring you joy and seem to bear fruit? Remember that discovering your gifts is a process.

---

4. How do you currently use your gifts to serve others?

Even if you haven't formally identified your gifts, how are you serving? In your church? Your workplace? Your family? Your community? If you're not currently serving, reflect on what's holding you back: fear, busyness, uncertainty, or something else?

Together Discussion:

1. How can our spiritual gifts complement each other in marriage?

After sharing your individual responses, discuss how your gifts might work together. Perhaps one of you has a teaching gift while the other has a gift of hospitality - together you could host a small group. Maybe one has mercy and the other has administration - you could serve effectively in a care ministry. Celebrate the unique ways God has designed you each and dream about how you'll serve both Him and the church together.

---

2. What role should the Holy Spirit play in our decision-making as a couple?

Discuss practical questions: How will we seek the Spirit's guidance when facing major decisions? What will we do if we sense the Spirit leading differently? How will we balance the Spirit's leading with practical wisdom and godly counsel? What does it look like to be "led by the Spirit" (Romans 8:14) in everyday married life?

3. How will we encourage each other's spiritual growth and development of gifts?

Be specific about how you'll support each other: Will you give each other time to serve in ministry? How will you handle it if ministry demands compete with family time? How will you encourage each other when you're discovering and developing gifts? How will you avoid the trap of one spouse's gifts being prioritized over the others?

Action Steps:

1. Take a spiritual gifts assessment together

Ask your facilitator for the New Beginnings Spiritual Gifts Test or find a reputable assessment online. Complete it individually, then compare and discuss your results. Remember that assessments are tools for exploration, not definitive diagnoses. Your actual experience in ministry will confirm your gifts over time.

2. Pray together asking God to reveal and develop your gifts

Set aside time to pray specifically about spiritual gifts. Ask the Holy Spirit to:

- Reveal the gifts He's given each of you
- Open doors for you to use those gifts
- Develop those gifts through practice and mentoring

- Help you serve with humility and love
- Give you unity as you minister together

---

3. Discuss how you want to minister together as a couple

Dream together about your ministry future: Do you want to serve in youth ministry together? Mentor younger couples? Be involved in missions? Use your home for hospitality? Lead a small group? Support a specific cause or organization? While your specific calling may not be clear yet, begin developing a shared vision for how your marriage can be a blessing to others and advance God's kingdom.

Closing Reflection: Becoming Whole in Christ

Understanding yourself as a spirit-soul-body unity indwelt by the Holy Spirit is not merely academic knowledge - it's transformative truth that can revolutionize your marriage. When you recognize that you're not merely managing personalities but nurturing whole persons with spiritual, emotional, and physical needs, you'll approach your relationship with greater wisdom and compassion.

As you prepare for marriage, commit to growing in all three dimensions: cultivating spiritual intimacy, developing emotional intelligence and stability, and caring for your physical bodies. Most importantly, remain continuously dependent on the Holy Spirit. It is only through His power that you'll be able to love as Christ loved, serve sacrificially, forgive quickly, and build a marriage that displays God's glory.

Prayer Suggestion:

"Holy Spirit, thank You for dwelling within us and making us new creations in Christ. We invite You to fill every part of us - our spirits, souls, and bodies. Sanctify us completely as we prepare for marriage. Reveal our spiritual gifts and show us how to serve together. Give us wisdom to care for each other's spiritual, emotional, and physical well-being. Help us to walk in step with You, sensitive to Your leading and empowered by Your presence. May our marriage be a testimony to Your transforming power. In Jesus' name, Amen."

CHAPTER 3: SHARING YOUR PERSONAL HISTORY

Introduction: The Courage to Be Known

One of the most beautiful and terrifying aspects of preparing for marriage is the invitation to be fully known. In our culture of carefully curated social media profiles and surface-level relationships, true vulnerability feels risky. Yet Proverbs 20:5 tells us, "Counsel in the heart of man is like deep water, but a man of understanding will draw it out."

Marriage requires this kind of drawing out - the courage to share your full story, including the chapters you'd rather skip. Your past relationships, your children, your family dynamics, and your unhealed wounds don't disappear when you say, "I do." They become part of the fabric of your marriage, for better or worse. The question is: Will you address them honestly now, or allow them to surface as hidden landmines later?

This chapter invites you into deeper waters. You'll discuss sensitive topics that require grace, honesty, and sometimes difficult conversations. Remember that transparency before marriage prevents painful surprises after marriage. God's design is for two people to become "one flesh" (Genesis 2:24), and true oneness requires knowing and being known completely.

As you work through this chapter, approach each other with the same grace Christ has shown you. Romans 15:7 instructs: "Accept one another, then, just as Christ accepted you, in order to bring praise to God." Your past does not disqualify you from a beautiful future - but your unwillingness to address it honestly might.

Part A: Past Relationships and Marriage History

Teaching: Understanding Your Relational History

Why Your Past Matters:

Some couples avoid discussing past relationships, thinking, "That's behind us now. Why dredge up old history?" However, your relational past has shaped who you are today. Past emotional relationships - including previous marriages – can create patterns, expectations, wounds, and sometimes ongoing obligations that will affect your upcoming marriage whether you acknowledge them or not.

The Bible takes past relationships seriously. Jesus addressed divorce and remarriage directly (Matthew 19:3-9), and Paul gave guidance about believers married to unbelievers (1 Corinthians 7:12-16). Scripture acknowledges that we live in a fallen world where marriages sometimes end, people carry wounds, and situations are complicated. God's grace is sufficient for every circumstance, but His grace doesn't erase consequences, eliminate the need for wisdom or eliminate the need for the Holy Spirit.

The Purpose of This Section:

This is not about judgment or shame. If you've been married before, God can redeem that experience and use it to make your marriage stronger. The goal here is:

- **Transparency**: Your future spouse deserves to know your full story
- **Healing**: Identifying areas where God's grace and healing are still needed
- **Wisdom**: Learning from past mistakes or sinful responses will help us to avoid repeating them
- **Practical planning**: Addressing any ongoing obligations or complications

Biblical Perspective on Divorce and Remarriage:

Churches hold different positions on divorce and remarriage, and a thorough treatment is beyond this workbook's scope. However, some biblical principles apply regardless of your theological position:

1. **God hates divorce** (Malachi 2:16), not because He wants to punish divorcees, but because He knows that divorce represents brokenness, pain, and the severing of a covenant He designed to reflect Christ and the church. God hates divorce because divorce hurts His children.

2. **Divorce happens for various reasons**, some more biblically justified than others. Jesus acknowledged adultery as grounds for divorce (Matthew 19:9). Paul addressed abandonment by an unbelieving spouse (1 Corinthians 7:15). Some Christian traditions also recognize abuse, addiction, or other covenant violations as "biblical grounds". Here is something you may want to consider: what sin can you commit that would nullify the healing power of Jesus' shed blood. Remember; our Father's goal is always repentance.
3. **Remarriage after divorce is possible** for believers, though churches differ on when and under what circumstances. If you're divorced and preparing to remarry, you should have worked through this issue with your pastor or church leadership before moving forward with engagement. If you haven't, now is a great time to do so.
4. **God specializes in redemption**. Whatever your history, God can take your broken pieces and create something beautiful. Joseph told his brothers, "You intended to harm me, but God intended it for good" (Genesis 50:20). This principle applies to painful divorces, too - God can bring good from this past pain. God can heal you of this past pain.

Lessons from the Past:

If you've been through divorce, you've likely learned painful but valuable lessons. Perhaps you learned:

- The importance of communication before resentment builds
- How unresolved conflict destroys intimacy
- The dangers of financial irresponsibility or dishonesty
- How neglecting the marriage relationship leads to "drifting"
- The impact of unaddressed mental health or addiction issues
- The necessity of shared values and spiritual alignment

These lessons, though gained through pain, can be "gifts" that can strengthen your upcoming marriage if you apply them wisely.

Ongoing Obligations:

Previous marriages sometimes create ongoing responsibilities:

- Child support or alimony payments
- Custody arrangements and co-parenting relationships
- Legal agreements or restrictions
- Emotional ties (especially if children are involved)

- Financial entanglements (shared property, debt, retirement accounts)

These aren't merely logistical issues. If they exist, they can be factors that will impact your new marriage practically, financially, and emotionally. Discussing them now demonstrates a personal maturity and can help protect your future marriage from tension or stress.

Individual Reflection (Complete privately first):

1. Have you been married before? If so, briefly describe the circumstances of the divorce.

You don't need to write a detailed account, but be honest about the basic facts: How long were you married? Were there children? What led to the breakdown of the marriage? Who initiated the divorce? Take responsibility for your part while being truthful about the circumstances. If you've never been married, simply note that and move to the next section.

---

2. What lessons did you learn from that experience?

Reflect deeply here. What would you do differently? What patterns or behaviors do you now recognize as unhealthy? What did you learn about yourself, both your strengths and weaknesses? How has that experience changed your approach to this upcoming marriage?

---

3. How has God brought healing to any past hurts?

Healing is a process, not an event. Describe your healing journey: Did you seek counseling? How did Scripture or the Christian community (your church) help? What specific areas has God healed? Are there areas where you're still healing? It's okay to acknowledge ongoing healing. The key is to be honest about where you are in the process.

---

4. Are there any ongoing legal or emotional obligations from previous relationships?

Be comprehensive and specific: child support amounts and duration, custody schedules, alimony agreements, shared property, ongoing legal matters, co-parenting communication requirements, or emotional ties that still require navigation. Your future spouse needs this information to enter marriage with their eyes open.

Sensitive Couple Discussion:

Preparing for This Conversation:

These discussions require special care. Before you begin:

- Pray together, asking God for grace, wisdom, and emotional safety
- Agree to listen without interrupting or becoming defensive
- Remember that past relationships ended – Your present relationship or marriage doesn't have to repeat those patterns
- Extend the grace you would want to receive
- If emotions become overwhelming, take a break and resume when calmer

1. Share your past relationship history with grace and honesty.

Take turns sharing what you wrote in your individual reflections. The listening partner's job is simply to listen, understand, and show compassion. Resist the temptation to judge, defend, or minimize. Ask clarifying questions gently: "Help me understand..." or "What was that experience like for you?"

Remember that your future spouse is trusting you with painful parts of their story. Honor that trust with kindness and confidentiality.

---

2. How can you support each other in areas where there's been past pain?

Discuss specific ways to provide support:

- "When I'm struggling with past memories, this is what helps me..."
- "If I seem triggered by something, I need you to..."
- "I'm working on healing in these areas, and your patience would help..."

- "Let's pray together about..."

Also discuss what kinds of support you cannot provide. If deep healing is needed, professional Christian counseling may be necessary. You can walk alongside your future spouse in their healing, but you cannot be their therapist.

---

3. Are there any practical matters (legal, financial, co-parenting) we need to plan for together?

Move from the emotional to the practical. Make a list of ongoing obligations and discuss how you'll navigate them:

- How will child support or alimony payments affect our budget?
- When will you need to communicate with your ex about the children, and how will we handle that?
- Are there legal restrictions we need to be aware of (custody limitations, relocation rules, etc.)?
- How will we handle it emotionally when you need to interact with your former spouse?
- What financial obligations will affect our ability to make future plans?

Write these down and create a plan together. This demonstrates that you're truly partners preparing to navigate these realities as a team.

Part B: Children—Present and Future

Teaching: Blended Families and Family Planning

The Biblical Perspective on Children:

Scripture presents children as gifts from God: "Behold, children are a heritage from the Lord, the fruit of the womb is a reward" (Psalm 127:3). God's design includes biological children within marriage, but His heart also extends to children who need families through adoption, fostering, or blended family situations.

When you marry someone with children from a previous relationship, you're not just gaining a spouse - you're joining an existing family system. This requires additional wisdom, patience, and grace beyond what first-time marriages require.

The Unique Challenges of Blended Families:

Blended families face distinct challenges:

- Children may resist the new marriage, feeling loyalty conflicts with their other biological parent
- Stepparents must earn authority and respect; they cannot simply assume it
- Different parenting styles and expectations can create conflict
- Ex-spouses remain in the picture, potentially causing tension
- Children may test boundaries to see if this new relationship will last or if they can capitalize on the previous relationship
- Biological parents may feel torn between protecting their children and building their new marriage

Despite these challenges, blended families can thrive when built on clear communication, realistic expectations, patience, and faith in God's redemptive purposes.

Principles for Stepparenting:

If you're becoming a stepparent, consider these biblical principles:

1. Love Without Demanding to Be Loved Jesus demonstrated unconditional love: "While we were still sinners, Christ died for us" (Romans 5:8). Stepchildren may not immediately reciprocate your love, and that's normal. Love them consistently without demanding emotional returns.

2. Support the Biological Parent's Authority Initially Especially at first, the biological parent should handle major discipline while you support them. As relationships develop and trust builds, your role can expand. Proverbs 15:1 reminds us: "A gentle answer turns away wrath, but a harsh word stirs up anger."

3. Build Relationship Before Exercising Authority Influence comes through relationship. Invest time getting to know your stepchildren, showing interest in their lives, and demonstrating reliability before expecting them to accept your authority. Watch for the "open door" and then step through.

4. Don't Replace the Other Biological Parent You're not trying to replace their mom or dad. You're an additional adult who loves and supports them. Respect the children's relationship with their other parent, even if that parent isn't perfect.

5. Maintain Unity with Your Spouse Never let children divide you. Present a united front on important issues, and don't let stepchildren manipulate you into taking sides against your spouse.

Planning for Biological Children Together:

If one or both of you have children from previous relationships, you'll need to discuss whether you'll have children together in this marriage. This decision carries emotional complexity:

- Children from previous relationships may worry about being displaced or loved less
- One spouse may desire more children while the other feels complete
- Age, health, or financial considerations may factor in
- Fair treatment of all children requires intentional planning

There's no single "right answer" here - this is a matter for prayer, honest discussion, and mutual agreement.

Parenting Styles and Values:

Even couples without previous children need to align on parenting philosophy before children arrive. Discuss:

- Discipline approaches (spanking, time-outs, consequences, etc.)
- Education preferences (public school, private school, homeschool)
- Screen time and technology boundaries
- Involvement in activities and sports
- Spiritual training and faith development
- Expectations for chores and responsibility

Major parenting conflicts often arise because couples never discussed these issues beforehand, assuming they'd naturally agree.

Current Family Situation:

1. Do either of you have children from previous relationships?

List each child: name, age, and current living situation. Provide basic information about their personality, interests, strengths, and any special needs or challenges.

2. If so, what are the custody arrangements and child support obligations?

Be specific about custody schedules: physical custody percentages, holiday arrangements, summer schedules, pickup/drop-off logistics, and child support amounts. Include details about who makes major decisions (legal custody) regarding education, healthcare, and religious upbringing.

3. How do your children feel about this upcoming marriage?

Have you talked with your children about the marriage? What was their response? Do they seem excited, anxious, resistant, or confused? Have they spent time with your future spouse? What's their current relationship like? Be honest—children's feelings matter and ignoring resistance won't make it disappear.

4. What will your role be as a stepparent?

This question is for the person becoming a stepparent. What are your expectations? What has the biological parent communicated about your role? What feels comfortable to you? What feels overwhelming? What boundaries need to be established?

Future Family Planning:

1. Do you want to have children together? How many?

Discuss your desires honestly. If you disagree, don't dismiss it as something you'll "figure out later." This is a major issue that requires planning and resolution before marriage. If one person absolutely wants children and the other absolutely doesn't, you may not be compatible for marriage.

---

2. What are your thoughts on timing for starting a family?

Consider: Do you want to wait a year or two to strengthen your marriage before adding children? Are there age, health, or financial factors that affect timing? If you already have children, do you want to allow time for blended family bonding before introducing new babies?

---

3. How will you blend parenting styles when you have children?

Identify areas where your parenting approaches differ and discuss how you'll navigate those differences. Will you adopt consistent rules across all children? How will you handle different expectations from the other biological parents? Who will discipline the children, and when?

---

4. What values and faith traditions do you want to pass on to your children?

Beyond practical parenting logistics, discuss the spiritual and moral foundation you want to establish. How will you incorporate faith, God, Jesus, into daily family life? What biblical values are non-negotiable for you? How will you disciple your children? What legacy do you want to leave?

Part C: Extended Family Relationships

Teaching: Leaving, Cleaving, and Honoring

The Biblical Foundation:

Genesis 2:24 provides God's blueprint for marriage: "Therefore a man shall leave his father and mother and be joined to his wife, and they shall become one flesh." This verse establishes three essential principles:

1. Leaving: Marriage requires leaving your family of origin psychologically, emotionally, and practically. You're no longer primarily a son or daughter - you're now someone's husband or wife. This doesn't mean abandoning your parents, but it does mean your primary loyalty shifts to your spouse.

2. Cleaving: The Hebrew word translated "joined" or "cleaving" means to cling, stick, or be glued together. It implies permanence, priority, and passionate commitment. Your spouse becomes your closest human relationship - closer than parents, siblings, hobbies or friends.

3. Becoming One: This unity encompasses physical, emotional, and spiritual dimensions. You're building a new family unit with its own identity, traditions, and boundaries.

The Tension: Leaving vs. Honoring:

Ephesians 6:2-3 commands: "Honor your father and mother, which is the first commandment with promise: that it may be well with you and you may live long on the earth." So how do you leave and cleave while still honoring parents?

The key is understanding that honoring doesn't mean obeying or allowing parents to control your marriage. As an adult, you honor parents by:

- Treating them with respect in how you speak to and about them
- Caring for them as they age (1 Timothy 5:4)
- Considering their counsel (though you make your own decisions)
- Including them appropriately in your life
- Not expecting them to meet needs only your spouse should meet

You dishonor parents by:

- Speaking disrespectfully or contemptuously about them
- Neglecting them when they have legitimate needs

- Deliberately excluding them from important life events to hurt them

However, establishing boundaries is not dishonoring. Healthy boundaries might include:

- Limiting how often parents can drop by unannounced
- Making decisions about your marriage, finances, and parenting without parental approval
- Choosing where you live, work, or worship based on your family's needs, not parents' preferences
- Declining to participate in unhealthy family dynamics

Common Extended Family Challenges:

Extended families can bless or burden a marriage. Common challenges include:

- **Intrusive parents** who offer unsolicited advice or expect constant access
- **Competing family traditions** that create holiday conflicts
- **Toxic family dynamics** involving manipulation, criticism, or favoritism
- **Unequal family involvement** where one spouse's family is much more engaged than the other's
- **Financial entanglements** where parents provide money with strings attached
- **Unresolved family conflicts** that predate the marriage but affect it
- **Cultural expectations** about family hierarchy or involvement that differ from biblical principles

The Solution: United Front:

The key to navigating extended family relationships is presenting a united front as a couple. Your spouse's concerns about your family should matter more than your family's opinions about your spouse. When you defend your spouse, establish boundaries together, and refuse to let family members divide you, you create a strong foundation for your marriage.

Family Background Assessment:

1. Describe your relationship with your parents and siblings.

How would you characterize your relationship with each parent: close, distant, conflicted, healthy, complicated? What about siblings? Are you tightly bonded or more independent? Do family members get along well, or is there tension? How often do you currently communicate with family members?

---

2. What family traditions are important to you?

Consider holidays, birthdays, reunions, weekly dinners, vacation patterns, religious observances, or unique family customs. Which traditions do you hope to continue in your marriage? Which ones are negotiable?

---

3. Are there any ongoing family conflicts or challenges?

Be honest about family dysfunction, mental health issues, addiction problems, long-standing feuds, personality conflicts, or toxic dynamics. Your future spouse needs to know what they're marrying into. This isn't about badmouthing family but about providing realistic expectations.

---

4. How involved do you want extended family to be in your marriage?

Consider: How often do you want to see extended family? How much input should they have in your decisions? What level of involvement feels comfortable versus intrusive? Are there areas where you want firm boundaries?

Planning Together:

1. How will we handle holidays and family gatherings?

Create a preliminary plan:

- Which holidays will you spend with which family (or alternate years)?

- Will you split holiday days between families or alternate entire holidays?
- Will you host holidays at your own home?
- How will you handle expectations when families live far apart or have conflicting celebrations?
- What will you do when families have hurt feelings about your decisions?

Remember that your plan can evolve, but establishing expectations upfront prevents holiday stress and family tension.

---

2. What boundaries might we need to establish with extended family?

Discuss potential boundaries:

- Communication expectations (calling before visiting, not showing up unannounced)
- Advice and criticism (how you'll handle unsolicited opinions about parenting, finances, etc.)
- Lending or borrowing money
- Holiday obligations
- Sharing personal information (keeping some things private between you)
- Access to your children (grandparent time, overnight visits)

Agree on boundaries together and support each other in maintaining them even when family pushes back.

---

3. How will we honor both families while building our own family identity?

Brainstorm ways to:

- Maintain connection with both families without being consumed by family obligations
- Create your own family traditions that are distinct from extended family
- Show respect and love while maintaining appropriate independence
- Navigate geographic distance if applicable
- Balance time with both families equitably
- Handle situations where one family is easier to be around than the other

Action Steps:

1. If children are involved, plan a family meeting to discuss the upcoming marriage, especially stepparent roles.

Schedule a time when everyone can be present and relaxed (not rushed). The biological parent should lead the conversation, but the future stepparent should participate. Topics to cover:

- "We're getting married because we love each other and want to build a life together"
- "This doesn't change how much I love you"
- "I'm not trying to replace your other parent"
- "I want to get to know you better and build a relationship with you"
- "Here's what will change..." (living arrangements, schedules, etc.)
- "Here's what will stay the same..."
- "Your feelings matter—you can talk to us about what you're feeling"

Allow children to ask questions and express concerns. Don't expect immediate enthusiasm but do establish that the decision is made and you're moving forward.

---

2. Discuss practical arrangements for child support, custody schedules, etc.

Create a written summary of:

- Custody schedule with dates, times, and transitions
- Child support or alimony amounts, payment schedules, and duration
- Legal agreements or court orders that govern arrangements
- How you'll communicate with ex-spouses (in person, text, email, co-parenting app)
- Boundaries around interactions with ex-spouses
- How you'll handle schedule changes or conflicts
- Financial planning that accounts for ongoing obligations

This becomes a reference document you can both access when questions arise.

---

3. Set preliminary boundaries and expectations for extended family relationships.

Have a conversation where you:

- Identify potential trouble spots with each family
- Agree on how you'll respond when boundaries are tested
- Discuss what you'll share and not share with extended family
- Establish communication patterns (who talks to whose family about what)
- Plan how you'll present decisions to family (together, united)
- Agree on a phrase or signal you'll use when one spouse needs the other to step in with family

Write down your agreements so you're on the same page and revisit them after marriage to adjust as needed.

Closing Reflection: The Gift of Honesty

Completing this chapter may have been emotionally exhausting. Believe me, I understand if that is true. Discussing past relationships, children, and family dynamics requires vulnerability and courage. But this investment of honesty now will pay dividends throughout your marriage. You've chosen to build on a foundation of truth rather than hiding difficult realities.

Remember that God is not intimidated by your past or your complicated family situations. He specializes in taking broken pieces and creating beautiful mosaics. Romans 8:28 promises: "And we know that all things work together for good to those who love God, to those who are the called according to Purpose."

As you move forward, continue choosing transparency over image management, honesty over false perfection, and grace over judgment. Congratulations! Your marriage will be stronger because you've done the hard work now.

Prayer Suggestion:

"Lord, thank You for the gift of grace that covers our past and redeems our stories. We give You our history. We give you the relationships that didn't work, the wounds we still carry, the children we love, and the families we come from. Help us to be wise and compassionate with each other as we navigate these complexities. Give us strength to establish healthy boundaries, wisdom to blend our families with love, and grace to honor extended family while building our own family identity. May our honesty with each other reflect the transparency You desire in relationship with us. Heal what needs healing and use our past experiences to make us better spouses. In Jesus' name, Amen."

CHAPTER 4: GOD'S DESIGN FOR MARRIAGE

Introduction: The Architect's Blueprint

When you purchase furniture that requires assembly, ignoring the manufacturer's instructions leads to frustration, wasted time, and a wobbly final product. Yet many couples approach marriage the same way - ignoring the Designer's instructions in favor of cultural patterns, family traditions, or personal preferences. The results are predictably unstable.

God didn't create marriage and then leave us to figure it out on our own. Throughout Scripture, He reveals His design with clarity and purpose. Marriage is not a human invention that evolved over time; it's a divine institution established in Eden before sin entered the world. God performed the first wedding ceremony, pronounced the first blessing on a married couple, and established the blueprint for how marriage should function.

But God's design for marriage is radically countercultural. In a world that prizes independence, God calls for covenant commitment. In a culture that emphasizes self-fulfillment, God calls for sacrificial service. In an age of gender confusion, God maintains distinct yet complementary roles for husbands and wives. Understanding and embracing God's design requires humility. Humility is the willingness to submit your expectations and preferences to His revealed will.

This chapter explores the biblical foundations of marriage: the covenant nature of the relationship, the husband's calling to love like Christ, the wife's calling to respect and support, and how these roles work together to create a covenant that displays God's glory. These truths may challenge your assumptions, but they offer the path to a marriage that reflects God's design and so experiences His blessings.

Truthfully, this is a lengthy chapter, but it is one of the most important in this study. Don't ignore it or turn from it because of its length. Go through the material a few pages each day in the coming week and thereby you'll be able to give it your full attention. Your future spouse will thank you in the end!

Part A: Marriage as a Sacred Covenant

Teaching: The Covenant Nature of Marriage

Understanding Covenant vs. Contract:

Read Malachi 2:14 together:

"Yet you say, 'For what reason?' Because the Lord has been the Witness between you and the wife of your youth, with whom you have dealt treacherously; yet she is your companion and your wife by covenant."

This verse reveals a fundamental truth: marriage is a covenant relationship with God as Witness. But what does "covenant" mean, and how is it different from a contract?

Contracts are:

- **Conditional**: "I'll do this if you do that"
- **Self-protective**: Designed to limit risk and ensure fairness
- **Performance-based**: Maintained as long as both parties fulfill obligations
- **Terminable**: Can be broken if terms are not met
- **Focused on rights**: "What am I entitled to?"
- **Limited in scope**: Covers specific agreed-upon terms
- **Legally enforceable**: But relationships often deteriorate once lawyers get involved

Covenants are:

- **Unconditional**: "I commit regardless of circumstances"
- **Self-giving**: Designed to create permanent unity
- **Character-based**: Maintained by faithfulness, not just performance
- **Permanent**: "Until death do us part"
- **Focused on responsibilities**: "What have I promised to give?"
- **Comprehensive in scope**: Covers all of life - "for better or worse, richer or poorer, in sickness and in health"
- **Sacred before God**: The ultimate Witness and guarantor

Biblical Covenants:

Throughout Scripture, God establishes covenants with His people—with Noah, Abraham, Moses, David, and ultimately through Christ in the New Covenant.

Each covenant reveals God's character: He is faithful, unchanging, and committed to His promises even when His people are unfaithful.

Marriage mirrors these Divine covenants. When God says in Malachi 2:14 that He is "witness" to your marriage covenant, He's not a passive observer. He's an active participant. Your vows are made before Him, and He holds you accountable to keep them. This is why Jesus said, "What God has joined together, let not man separate" (Matthew 19:6). God Himself joins husband and wife in the marriage covenant.

Why Covenant Matters in Modern Marriage:

Our culture has reduced marriage to a contract: "As long as I'm happy, fulfilled, and getting what I need, I'll stay married." When these conditions aren't met, people feel justified in breaking the contract. And rightly so. Contracts can and are broken. This contractual mindset has led to rampant divorce, serial marriages, and the normalization of "trading up" for a better spouse.

But covenant thinking transforms marriage:

- When you view marriage as a covenant, you don't bail when things get hard - you dig deeper
- You don't keep score of who's doing more - you both give every ounce of 100%
- You don't threaten divorce during arguments - divorce is never an option
- You don't love conditionally based on performance - you love based on commitment
- You don't protect your individual interests - you prioritize the unity of the marriage and the interests of your spouse

This doesn't mean staying in abusive situations (safety matters and God doesn't require anyone to remain in danger). But it does mean that the typical reasons people divorce - "we grew apart," "I'm not happy anymore," "we want different things" - are not valid reasons to break one's covenant.

The Cost and Beauty of Covenant:

Covenant is costly. It requires dying to self (Galatians 2:20), putting your spouse's needs above your preferences (Philippians 2:3-4), and persevering through seasons of difficulty. But covenant is also beautiful. It creates safety, depth, intimacy and a security that contractual relationships can never achieve. When you know your spouse will never leave, you can be fully vulnerable.

When you trust their commitment is permanent, you can weather any storm together.

The Covenant Triangle:

Individual Study:

Draw a triangle on a piece of paper. Place "God" at the top point, your name at the bottom left corner, and your fiancé's name at the bottom right corner. This simple diagram illustrates a profound truth about the Covenant of Marriage.

The Geometry of Covenant:

Notice what happens in this triangle:

- As you move closer to God (traveling up your side of the triangle), you simultaneously move closer to your spouse
- The closer you both get to God, the closer you get to each other
- If one person moves away from God (down the triangle), the distance between you and your spouse increases
- God is not peripheral to your marriage - He is the apex that holds it together

This isn't just a nice illustration; it's a spiritual reality. When both partners are pursuing God individually, their marriage naturally strengthens. When either partner drifts from God, the marriage suffers even if the other partner is spiritually healthy.

Reflection Questions:

1. How does God's presence strengthen your relationship with each other?

Consider: How does your shared faith provide a foundation? How does praying together impact your unity? How does Scripture offer wisdom for marriage challenges? How does God's presence give you grace to forgive and persevere?

2. What happens when one person moves away from God in this triangle?

Reflect on times when you've been spiritually distant from God. How did it affect your relationships? What might happen in your marriage if one of you stops pursuing God—becomes bitter, turns to sin, or simply becomes spiritually apathetic? How would this impact the other spouse and the marriage?

Couple Discussion:

1. How will we keep God at the center of our marriage?

Discuss specific, practical commitments:

- Will we pray together daily? When and for how long?
- Will we read Scripture together? What approach will we take?
- Will we attend church together faithfully? Small group? Bible study?
- Will we serve together in ministry?
- How will we make spiritual conversations a natural part of daily life?
- Will we have regular spiritual check-ins: "How's your walk with God?"
- How will we handle it when one of us is struggling spiritually?

Make these commitments concrete and sustainable. Better to start small and be consistent than to set unrealistic expectations you won't maintain.

---

2. What practices will help us maintain our covenant relationship?

Beyond spiritual disciplines, discuss:

- How will we protect time together despite busy schedules?
- What boundaries will we establish around work, hobbies, and friendships to prioritize our marriage?
- How will we handle conflict without threatening our covenant?
- Will we agree never to use the word "divorce" in arguments?
- How will we regularly renew our commitment to each other?
- What will we do when one of us is struggling to keep covenant commitments?

3. How can we remind each other of our covenant commitment during difficult times?

Brainstorm specific reminders:

- Keep your wedding vows where you can see them
- Celebrate your anniversary meaningfully each year
- Revisit this workbook periodically to remember your pre-marriage commitments
- Speak your commitment aloud during conflicts: "I'm committed to you no matter what"
- Pray together about challenges, reminding each other that God is the third strand (Ecclesiastes 4:12)
- Seek help early when problems arise rather than letting resentment build

---

Part B: The Husband's Calling

Teaching: Christ-Like Love and Servant Leadership

Biblical Foundation: Read Ephesians 5:25-33 together

"Husbands, love your wives, just as Christ also loved the church and gave Himself for her, that He might sanctify and cleanse her with the washing of water by the word, that He might present her to Himself a glorious church, not having spot or wrinkle or any such thing, but that she should be holy and without blemish. So, husbands ought to love their own wives as their own bodies; he who loves his wife loves himself. For no one ever hated his own flesh, but nourishes and cherishes it, just as the Lord does the church. For we are members of His body, of His flesh and of His bones. 'For this reason, a man shall leave his father and mother and be joined to his wife, and the two shall become one flesh.' This is a great mystery, but I speak concerning Christ and the church. Nevertheless, let each one of you in particular so love his own wife as himself, and let the wife see that she respects her husband."

The Husband's High Calling:

When discussing biblical marriage roles, much attention is often given to the wife's role of submission. But notice where Paul begins? He with the husband's responsibility to love his wife like Christ loves the church. This is not a convenient starting point. It is the foundation of a biblical marriage. The husband's calling is actually more demanding, more sacrificial, and more clearly defined than the wife's. Why? Because as Christ is the spiritual head of the church, the husband is the spiritual head of the home.

What Christ-Like Love Looks Like:

Paul doesn't give husbands multiple options for how to love their wives. There's one standard: "as Christ loved the church." This is the highest possible standard because Christ's love for the church was:

1. Sacrificial Love (v. 25): "gave Himself for her"

Christ didn't give gifts to the church; He gave Himself. He didn't love when it was convenient or when the church deserved it. He loved at the cost of His own life. For husbands, this means:

- Putting your wife's needs above your own desires
- Sacrificing your time, comfort, and preferences for her well-being
- Being willing to give up anything - career advancement, hobbies, even your life - for her sake
- Loving even when she's unlovable, ungrateful, or difficult

This eliminates any notion of selfish leadership or using authority for personal benefit.

2. Sanctifying Love (v. 26-27): "that He might sanctify and cleanse her"

Christ's love has a purpose: to make the church holy. Similarly, a husband's love should help his wife grow spiritually and become more like Christ. This means:

- Praying for her spiritual growth
- Encouraging her relationship with God
- Speaking truth lovingly when she needs correction or encouragement
- Creating an environment where she can flourish spiritually
- Protecting her from sin and negative influences
- Leading by example in pursuing holiness

This is not about controlling her or demanding perfection, but about lovingly nurturing her spiritual growth.

3. Nourishing Love (v. 29): "nourishes and cherishes it"

"Nourish" means to feed, sustain, and promote growth - like caring for your own body. "Cherish" means to warm, protect, and treat as precious. Husbands should:

- Provide for their wife's physical, emotional, and spiritual needs
- Protect her from harm, disrespect, and unnecessary hardship
- Treat her as precious and valuable
- Notice what she needs and proactively meet those needs
- Create a safe, warm environment where she feels loved and valued

4. One-Flesh Love (v. 28, 31): "love their own wives as their own bodies"

Because husband and wife are one flesh, loving your wife is literally loving yourself. What benefits her benefits you. What harms her harms you. This creates:

- Unity of purpose and direction
- Interdependence rather than independence
- Shared joys and shared sorrows
- Mutual care and concern
- The impossibility of true selfishness - her good is your good

Spiritual Leadership Redefined:

Many men misunderstand spiritual leadership, thinking it means:

- Making all decisions unilaterally
- Demanding obedience
- Having final say in every matter
- Being served by their wife
- Dominating the relationship

But Christ-patterned spiritual leadership looks different. Jesus said, "Whoever desires to become great among you, let him be your servant. And whoever desires to be first among you, let him be your slave - just as the Son of Man did not come to be served, but to serve" (Matthew 20:26-28).

True spiritual leadership means:

- Taking responsibility for the spiritual climate of your home
- God honoring by: Initiating prayer, Bible reading, and spiritual dialogues
- Leading by example, not just by directive
- Serving sacrificially, not demanding service
- Making decisions with your wife's input and welfare in mind
- Taking ownership when things go wrong rather than blaming
- Creating space for your wife's gifts and contributions
- Seeking wisdom from God and godly counsel
- Apologizing and changing when you're wrong

Spiritual leadership is not about authority for its own sake - it's about taking responsibility for the well-being and spiritual health of your marriage and family.

Individual Reflection for Men:

1. "Husbands, love your wives as Christ loved the church." What does this kind of love look like practically?

Be specific. List concrete actions: How will you demonstrate sacrificial love daily? Weekly? In times of conflict? When you're tired or stressed? What will loving like Christ cost you personally? What habits or attitudes need to change?

---

2. How did Christ demonstrate His love for the church?

Study the Gospels and note specific examples: Jesus washing the disciples' feet (John 13), Jesus praying for His disciples (John 17), Jesus enduring the cross (Hebrews 12:2), Jesus interceding for us now (Hebrews 7:25). What principles can you extract from Christ's example and apply to loving your wife?

---

3. What does it mean to be the spiritual leader of your home?

Reflect honestly: Does this excite you or intimidate you? What does spiritual leadership look like in daily life—not just Sundays, but Monday through Saturday? What will it require of you? Where do you need to grow to lead well?

What specific spiritual disciplines will you need to maintain to lead from spiritual strength rather than emptiness?

4. How can you love your wife in a way that helps her flourish?

Think about your fiancée specifically: What makes her feel loved? What helps her grow? What stifles her? How can you create an environment where her gifts emerge and her relationship with God deepens? What obstacles might you need to remove?

Discussion Questions:

For the wife to answer, for both to discuss:

1. How do you want your husband to show Christ-like love to you?

Wives, be specific and honest about what makes you feel loved, valued, and cherished. Help your future husband understand your needs. This isn't demanding or selfish - it's giving him a roadmap to follow in loving you.

2. What does biblical leadership look like in everyday decisions?

Discuss how decisions will be made:

- Will you discuss everything together first?
- When will he need to make a final decision, and when is consensus necessary?
- How will he lead without dismissing your input?
- What's the difference between leadership and domination?
- How should he lead when you have different perspectives?

3. How can we make sure leadership doesn't become domination?

Establish safeguards:

- What accountability will he have outside the marriage?
- How can you raise concerns if you feel unheard or disrespected?
- What does mutual submission (Ephesians 5:21) look like alongside male headship?
- How will you both ensure decisions are made in love, not selfishness?

Part C: The Wife's Calling

Teaching: Biblical Submission and Helper Design

Biblical Foundation: Read 1 Peter 3:1-7 together

"Wives, likewise, be submissive to your own husbands, so that even if some do not obey the Word, they, without a word, may be won by the conduct of their wives, when they observe your chaste conduct. Do not let your adornment be merely outward - arranging the hair, wearing gold, or putting on fine apparel - rather let it be the hidden person of the heart, with the incorruptible beauty of a gentle and quiet spirit, which is very precious in the sight of God. For in this manner, in former times, the holy women who trusted in God also adorned themselves, being submissive to their own husbands, as Sarah obeyed Abraham, calling him lord, and whose daughters you are if you do good and are not afraid with any terror. Husbands, likewise (in the same way), dwell with them with understanding, giving honor to the wife, as to the weaker vessel, and as being heirs together of the grace of life, that your prayers may not be hindered."

Reclaiming Biblical Submission:

Few biblical concepts are more misunderstood or maligned than wifely submission. Modern culture hears "submission" and thinks: doormat, inferiority, oppression, abuse. Even in the church, submission has been twisted to justify ungodly male domination. But biblical submission is none of these things.

What Submission Is NOT:

- Inferiority (men and women are equally created in God's image - Genesis 1:27)
- Silence (godly women throughout Scripture spoke truth courageously)
- Blind obedience (wives are not required to follow husbands into sin)

- Accepting abuse (God never requires anyone to submit to physical, emotional, or spiritual abuse)
- Slavery or servitude (wives are partners, not servants)
- Permission for husbands to neglect their responsibilities
- A justification for male selfishness or domination

What Submission IS:

The Greek word for "submit" (hypotassō) is actually a military term meaning "to arrange under." It's a voluntary positioning of yourself under another's authority - not because you're inferior, but for the sake of order, unity, and function.

1. Submission is Voluntary Notice that Paul addresses wives directly: "Wives, submit..." He doesn't tell husbands, "Make your wives submit." Submission is a choice a wife makes, not something a husband enforces. A husband who demands submission has fundamentally misunderstood the concept and is out of fellowship with God's plan for their marriage.

2. Submission is Role-Based, Not Value-Based In God's economy, different roles never indicate different value. The Father, Son, and Holy Spirit are co-equal in the Trinity, yet the Son submits to the Father's will (John 6:38, Philippians 2:5-8). Jesus' submission didn't make Him inferior - it demonstrated the beauty of functional order within the perfect unity of the Trinity.

Similarly, a wife's submission to her husband doesn't make her inferior - it reflects God's design for order and leadership within the marriage covenant.

3. Submission is Trusting God's Design First Peter 3:5 says holy women "trusted in God" and therefore submitted to their husbands. Submission is fundamentally an act of faith - trusting that God's design is good even when it's countercultural. It's believing that God will honor the wife's obedience to God's principles even if her husband doesn't lead perfectly.

4. Submission Has Limits Wives submit to their "own husbands" (not to men in general) and even then, submission to God takes priority. Acts 5:29 establishes the principle: "We ought to obey God rather than men." If a husband asks his wife to sin, lie, or violate Scripture, her submission to God overrides submission to her husband.

5. Submission is Respect in Action Ephesians 5:33 summarizes: "Let the wife see that she respects her husband." Submission is the practical outworking of respect. It means:

- Honoring his leadership even when you disagree
- Speaking respectfully to him and about him
- Supporting his decisions after you've given input
- Building him up rather than tearing him down either in words or actions
- Trusting his judgment in his areas of responsibility
- Following his lead in spiritual matters

The Helper Design:

Before sin entered the world, God said, "It is not good that man should be alone; I will make him a helper comparable to him" (Genesis 2:18). "Helper" here doesn't mean "servant" or "assistant." The Hebrew word "ezer" is used most often in Scripture to describe God Himself as our helper (Psalm 33:20, 70:5, 115:9-11). It means "strong helper" or "rescuer." It is never used to describe a subservient position.

What Being a Helper Means:

1. Complementarity "Comparable to him" literally means "corresponding to" or "completing." A wife completes what's lacking in her husband - not because he's deficient, but because God's design involves complementary strengths. Where he's weak, she's strong. Where he's strong, she's strong in different ways.

2. Strategic Support A good helper doesn't just follow orders - she brings insight, wisdom, and perspective that the leader might miss. Proverbs 31 describes a wife who manages household affairs, engages in business, makes decisions about property, and speaks with wisdom. She's not passive - she's proactively helping her household flourish.

3. Influence Wives have profound influence over their husbands. First Peter 3:1 says husbands "may be won" by their wives' conduct. Proverbs 31:11-12 says her husband's heart "safely trusts her" and "she does him good and not evil all the days of her life." A wife's influence can draw her husband toward God or away from Him.

4. Partnership Genesis 2:18 doesn't establish hierarchy - that comes after the fall (Genesis 3:16). God's original design was partnership with complementary roles. A wife is not beneath her husband; she's beside him, working toward shared goals with different but equally valuable contributions. Remember: Eve was taken from Adam's "side" not his "back."

Individual Reflection for Women:

1. What does biblical submission look like in a healthy marriage?

Paint a picture: What would submission look like in your future daily life? In decision-making? In conflict? How can you submit while still being yourself - strong, gifted, intelligent, and opinionated? What examples have you seen of healthy submission? What examples have you seen of unhealthy versions that aren't truly biblical?

2. How is submission different from being a doormat?

A doormat has no voice, no opinions, and no boundaries. How is biblical submission different? Let's brain storm: Where do you draw the line? When should you respectfully disagree? When should you defer? How can you maintain your identity and dignity while honoring your husband's leadership?

3. What does it mean to be a "helper" according to Genesis 2:18?

Reflect on the strength inherent in the term "helper." How have you already helped your fiancé? Where are you strong where he's weak? What unique insights, gifts, or perspectives do you bring to the relationship? How will you use your influence for good in your marriage?

4. How can you use your influence to encourage your husband's spiritual growth?

Consider: How does your respect (or lack of it) affect him spiritually? How can your prayers support him? How can you encourage him toward godliness without nagging? What role will you play in holding him accountable to his spiritual responsibilities?

For Husbands - 1 Peter 3:7:

Teaching: Honoring Your Wife

"Husbands, likewise, dwell with them with understanding, giving honor to the wife, as to the weaker vessel, and as being heirs together of the grace of life, that your prayers may not be hindered."

Notice that Peter says "likewise"- meaning husbands have responsibilities just as wives do. Two commands stand out:

1. Dwell with Understanding "Dwell with" means to live together intimately, knowing her deeply. "Understanding" means gaining knowledge. Husbands must:

- Study their wives - learn what she needs, what she fears, what she dreams
- Listen actively when she talks
- Notice her emotional state and respond with compassion
- Understand her differently than you understand yourself
- Ask questions rather than making assumptions
- Remember what matters to her

2. Give Honor "Honor" means to assign value, show respect, treat as precious. Husbands should:

- Speak respectfully to her and about her (never belittle or mock)
- Protect her reputation – both inside the home and outside the home
- Value her opinions and input
- Treat her as a co-heir of grace - equal in spiritual standing
- Never use "weaker vessel" as an excuse to dominate; use it as a reason to be gentle, protective and to uphold
- Recognize that dishonoring her hinders your prayers - your relationship with God suffers when you mistreat your wife

Reflection Questions for Men:

1. What does it mean to "dwell with understanding"?

How well do you currently know your fiancée? What efforts will you make to keep understanding her after marriage when the newness wears off? How will you stay curious about her thoughts, feelings, and needs?

2. How does dishonoring your wife affect your relationship with God?

This verse says your prayers are hindered when you don't honor your wife. Why is God so concerned about how you treat her? What does this reveal about God's view of marriage? What specific behaviors would constitute dishonoring her?

Couple Discussion: (Talk it over!)

1. How do we both submit to God's design while honoring each other's gifts?

Discuss how to implement biblical roles without stifling either person's gifts, personality, or contributions. How will you balance leadership and submission with mutual respect and partnership?

---

2. What does mutual respect look like in our relationship?

Ephesians 5:21 calls for "submitting to one another in the fear of God" before giving specific instructions to wives and husbands. Discuss:

- How does mutual submission coexist with male headship?
- What does respect look like practically (tone, words, actions)?
- How will you show respect even during disagreements?
- What behaviors would violate respect for each other?

---

3. How can we support each other's calling while fulfilling our own?

You're both called to specific roles in marriage, but also to individual callings (career, ministry, personal development). Discuss:

- How will you encourage each other's gifts and callings?
- When might role-based responsibilities conflict with individual callings?
- How will you make decisions about career opportunities, ministry commitments, or educational pursuits?
- How can you be each other's biggest champion?

Part D: Living Out Your Roles Together

Teaching: From Theory to Practice

Understanding biblical roles is one thing; living them out daily is another. Theory is neat and clean. **Real life is messy**. You'll have days when husbands don't feel like leading sacrificially and wives don't feel like following respectfully. You'll face situations where the "right" decision isn't clear. You'll discover that your personalities, backgrounds, and temperaments create unique challenges in implementing these roles.

The goal is not robotic adherence to a formula, but a grace-filled partnership where both spouses humbly seek to honor God's design while extending grace when you fail (and you will).

Key Principles for Living Out Your Roles:

1. Lead with Humility, Follow with Grace Husbands should lead humbly, inviting input and admitting when they're wrong. Wives should follow graciously, supporting decisions even when they would have chosen differently, while respectfully voicing concerns when necessary.

2. Major on Unity, Minor on Methods Unity matters more than winning arguments about how to implement roles. Stay flexible about methods while remaining committed to biblical principles.

3. Play to Your Strengths While maintaining biblical roles, recognize each other's strengths and let those guide practical task division. If she's better with finances, she can manage them under his oversight. If he's more organized with schedules, he can coordinate calendars. Biblical roles don't require rigid task assignments.

4. Give Grace for Growth Neither of you will perfectly fulfill your roles. Give grace, encourage progress, and avoid scorekeeping. Remember you're both learning together.

5. Seek Help When Stuck If you struggle to implement biblical roles healthily, seek godly counsel. Don't let pride prevent you from getting help.

Practical Application:

1. In what areas do you naturally complement each other?

Identify your complementary strengths: Is one more analytical while the other is more intuitive? Is one a big-picture thinker while the other notices details? Is one more social while the other is more reflective? Celebrate these differences and discuss how they'll strengthen your marriage.

2. How will you handle decisions when you disagree?

Establish a decision-making process:

- *Discuss thoroughly, listening to each other's perspectives*
- *Pray together about the decision*
- *Seek godly counsel if needed*
- *If consensus can't be reached, the husband makes the final decision*
- *Both commit to supporting the decision once it's made*
- *Agree to revisit and adjust if the decision proves unwise*

Also discuss: What types of decisions require mutual agreement (major purchases, parenting decisions)? What decisions can be made individually?

---

3. What will daily spiritual leadership look like in your home?

Be specific about "spiritual rhythms:"

- *Will you pray together at breakfast? Before bed? Both?*
- *Will you read Scripture together? When and how?*
- *Will you have weekly spiritual conversations checking in on each other's walk with God?*
- *How will you disciple future children?*
- *What will Sundays look like spiritually?*

Remember: Spiritual leadership isn't complicated. It consistently initiates spiritual activities and conversations.

---

4. How will you maintain unity while respecting your different roles?

Discuss how to avoid common pitfalls:

- *Husbands: How will you avoid dictatorial leadership that dismisses her input?*
- *Wives: How will you avoid manipulative submission that undermines his leadership?*
- *Both: How will you ensure biblical roles strengthen rather than damage your unity?*
- *What signals will you use when one person feels the balance is off?*

Action Steps:

1. Write out your personal commitment to your biblical role in marriage

Each person should write a personal statement committing to their biblical role. This isn't a contract with each other - it's a covenant commitment to God about how you'll approach your role in marriage.

For Husbands, include:

- Commitment to love sacrificially like Christ
- Commitment to spiritual leadership through example and initiation
- Commitment to honor, cherish, and dwell with understanding
- Specific areas where you know you'll need God's help

For Wives, include:

- Commitment to respect and support your husband's leadership
- Commitment to be a strong helper using your gifts for your marriage's good
- Commitment to influence him toward godliness
- Specific areas where you know you'll need God's help

Keep these statements and revisit them periodically throughout your marriage.

2. Pray together about how God wants you to serve Him as a married couple

Set aside extended time to pray specifically about:

- Your marriage as a testimony to Christ and the church
- How you'll use your complementary roles to advance God's kingdom
- Ministry opportunities you might pursue together
- How God wants to use your marriage to bless others
- Wisdom to implement biblical roles in your unique relationship
- Humility to submit to God's design even when it's countercultural

---

3. Discuss specific ways you want to honor God through your marriage

Brainstorm concrete ways your marriage will display God's glory:

- Hospitality: How will you use your home to bless others?
- Ministry: What specific service opportunities interest you both?
- Generosity: How will you use your resources to support God's kingdom?
- Testimony: How will unbelievers see Christ through your marriage?
- Mentoring: Will you invest in younger couples once you're established?
- Parenting: How will you raise children who know and love God?

Dream together about the legacy you want to build.

Closing Reflection: The Beauty of God's Design

God's design for marriage is a covenant commitment, Christ-like husband love, respectful wife submission, and complementary partnership and is countercultural, challenging, and beautiful. It requires death to self, humility, and ongoing dependence on the Holy Spirit. You cannot live out these roles in your own strength.

But when husband and wife embrace God's design, marriage becomes a living picture of the gospel. Ephesians 5:32 says, "This is a great mystery, but I speak concerning Christ and the church." Your marriage is meant to display Christ's relationship with the church - His sacrificial love, the church's joyful submission, and the unity that results.

As you prepare to say, "I do," remember that you're not just promising to love each other. You're accepting God's calling to represent the gospel through your marriage. This calling is higher than mere happiness - it's about holiness and God's glory. And paradoxically, when you pursue God's glory through biblical marriage, you'll discover the deep satisfaction and joy that come from living according to your Creator's design.

Prayer Suggestion:

"Father, Your design for marriage is higher and more beautiful than we can fully comprehend. Help us to embrace biblical roles with humility and grace. Give [husband's name] strength to love sacrificially like Christ, to lead with wisdom and servanthood, and to cherish and honor his wife. Give [wife's name] strength to respect and support her husband's leadership, to be a strong helper, and to use her influence for his spiritual good. Help us both to maintain unity while honoring our different roles. When we fail give us grace to forgive quickly and grow together. May our marriage be a testimony to Your love for each of us, Your gospel, and constantly displaying Christ's love for the church. We commit our marriage covenant to You, the faithful Witness and keeper of all promises. In Jesus' name, Amen."

Final Thought:

You've now explored God's design for marriage in depth. Before moving to the next chapter, take time to discuss any questions, concerns, or areas where you need clarity. If you find yourselves disagreeing about these biblical roles, don't ignore the disagreement - address it now with your pastor or a trusted mentor. Unity on these foundational issues will serve you well throughout your marriage. Remember that understanding God's design is a lifelong journey, and you don't need to have it all figured out perfectly before you marry. What matters is that you're both committed to pursuing God's design together, with humility and grace for the learning process ahead.

CHAPTER 5: UNDERSTANDING EACH OTHER'S PERSONALITY

Introduction: Fearfully and Wonderfully Made

"I will praise You, for I am fearfully and wonderfully made; marvelous are Your works, and that my soul knows very well" (Psalm 139:14). David's declaration of wonder at God's creative design applies not just to the physical body, but to the intricate ways God has wired each person's personality, temperament, and psychological makeup.

You are marrying someone who is fundamentally different from you. Even couples who seem remarkably similar discover profound differences once they live together. For instance: He processes decisions slowly and deliberately; she decides quickly and intuitively. She needs social interaction to recharge; he needs solitude. He's comfortable with spontaneity; she thrives on planning. He focuses on tasks; she focuses on relationships. These differences aren't defects. The differences are part of our design – how the Father has "wired us together."

Many couples enter marriage expecting their spouse to think, feel, and process life exactly as they do or worse – in a certain way. When reality hits - when she's still talking and he wants silence, when he's ready to decide and she needs more time, when she wants to attend every social event and he wants to stay home - disappointment and conflict can arise. The temptation is strong to "fix" one's spouse, to reshape them into your image rather than appreciating God's image in them!

This chapter will help you understand the unique way God has designed each of you, learn to appreciate rather than merely tolerate your individual differences, and discover how your complementary personalities can strengthen rather than strain your marriage. You'll explore why change must come from God rather than your efforts to reform your spouse, and you'll develop practical strategies for navigating personality differences with grace and wisdom.

The goal isn't to eliminate differences - that's neither possible, desirable nor realistic. The goal is to understand, appreciate, and leverage your differences so that together you're stronger as a couple than either of you could be alone.

Part A: Discovering Your Unique Design

Teaching: The Biblical Foundation for Personality Differences

Created for Diversity:

From the opening chapters of Genesis, we see God's love for diversity. He didn't create one type of tree, one species of bird, or one kind of flower. He created breathtaking variety. Similarly, God didn't create one personality template for all humanity. He fashioned each person with unique combinations of traits, strengths, weaknesses, and tendencies.

This diversity reflects God's own nature. The Trinity itself demonstrates unity within diversity - three distinct Persons, one God. The Father, Son, and Holy Spirit have different roles and relate to creation differently, yet they're perfectly unified in essence, will, and purpose. Your marriage is meant to reflect this same dynamic: two distinct persons, unified in covenant with different roles.

Personality and Sanctification:

It's crucial to distinguish between personality and character. Your personality includes traits like introversion/extroversion, thinking/feeling preferences, and organizational style. These traits are largely innate - part of how God has wired you together - and they're morally neutral. Your character, however, includes qualities like honesty, kindness, self-control, and faithfulness. These are cultivated through sanctification and are matters of spiritual maturity.

God doesn't intend to erase your personality through sanctification. He redeems it. An introvert doesn't need to become an extrovert to be godly, and an extrovert doesn't need to become reserved. But both need to develop character qualities like love, patience, and self-control within their natural temperament.

Why Understanding Personality Matters:

Understanding personality differences helps you:

1. **Stop Taking Things Personally**: When you realize your spouse's quietness after work isn't rejection but introversion, or their constant questions aren't criticism but their processing style, you stop interpreting differences as offenses.

2. **Communicate More Effectively**: Different personalities communicate differently. Understanding your spouse's style helps you speak their language.
3. **Reduce Unnecessary Conflict**: Many marital conflicts stem from personality clashes, not moral issues. Recognizing this reduces conflict.
4. **Appreciate Rather Than Criticize**: What initially attracts us (their confidence, their warmth, their organization) can later irritate us. Understanding helps maintain appreciation.
5. **Collaborate More Effectively**: When you understand each other's strengths and limitations, you can divide responsibilities wisely and work together more smoothly.

Personality Frameworks:

Various personality assessments exist—Myers-Briggs, DISC, Enneagram, Big Five, StrengthsFinder, and others. While no assessment perfectly captures human complexity, these tools provide vocabulary for discussing differences and insight into patterns. Your advisor may administer a specific assessment, or you might explore several to gain comprehensive understanding.

Remember that personality assessments are descriptive, not prescriptive. They describe tendencies, not destinies. You're not locked into your personality type, and you shouldn't use your personality as an excuse for sin or selfishness ("That's just how I am!"). Instead, use these insights as starting points for understanding and growth.

Before You Begin:

Complete the Personal Style Inventory (provided separately and administered by your Facilitator)

Take the assessment individually before reading your partner's results. Answer honestly based on who you actually are, not who you wish you were or think you should be. There are no "right" answers - only accurate or inaccurate self-awareness.

Understanding the Results Together:

After both of you have completed the assessment, allow your facilitator to help share your results with each other. Approach this conversation with curiosity and openness, not judgment or defensiveness.

1. What did you learn about your own personality style?

Reflect on your results: Did the assessment accurately capture how you see yourself? What aspects resonated strongly? Were there any elements that didn't quite fit? What language or categories helped you understand yourself better? Did the assessment validate things you already knew, or did it reveal blind spots?

---

2. What surprised you most about your results?

Consider: Were there traits you didn't realize about yourself? Did the assessment challenge any self-perceptions? Did you discover motivations you hadn't recognized? Were there strengths you've undervalued or weaknesses you've overlooked?

---

3. How do you see your personality strengths in everyday life?

Give concrete examples: How do your natural strengths show up at work? In friendships? In how you handle stress? In decision-making? In social situations? How have these strengths helped you succeed or navigate challenges? Be specific about situations where your personality served you well.

---

4. What challenges does your personality style sometimes create?

Be honest about limitations: When does your natural style cause problems? What situations exhaust you? Where do you tend to struggle? How might your strengths become weaknesses when overused? (For example: confidence can become arrogance, thoroughness can become perfectionism, spontaneity can become irresponsibility.) What areas require extra effort for you?

Part B: Accepting Your Differences

Teaching: The Dangerous "Fixer" Mentality

Biblical Foundation: Read 1 Corinthians 12:4-7 together

"There are diversities of gifts, but the same Spirit. There are differences of ministries, but the same Lord. And there are diversities of activities, but it is the same God who works all in all. But the manifestation of the Spirit is given to each one for the profit of all."

It is obvious that Paul is addressing the church at Corinth in the above citation, but the biblical principle applies to marriage as well: diversity is by Divine design, and differences are for mutual benefit. Just as the body needs different parts with different functions (1 Corinthians 12:14-27), your marriage needs each of your individual diverse personalities working in unity.

The "Fixer" Temptation:

One of the most common - and damaging - patterns in marriage is the "fixer" mentality. The "fixer" mentality describes the belief that it's your job to change your spouse into a better (read: more like your) version of themselves. This mentality sounds noble: "I just want to help them grow!" But underneath often lurks self-pride, self-control, and a fundamental rejection of how God made your spouse.

Why We Try to "Fix" Our Spouses:

1. **Discomfort with Differences**: Your spouse's different approach to life creates discomfort. Rather than adapting, you pressure them to change.
2. **Belief in Your Own Superiority**: Deep down, you think your way is the right way. If they'd just do things your way, everything would be better.
3. **Anxiety and Control**: Their differences create unpredictability. Changing them gives you a sense of control.
4. **Unmet Expectations**: They're not who you expected them to be, so you're trying to mold them into your ideal.
5. **Genuine Concern Mixed with Pride**: You may genuinely want them to grow, but you've confused your preferences with God's will.

The Problem with "Fixing":

When you try to change your spouse, you:

- Communicate that they're not acceptable as they are
- Position yourself as superior judge of what they need
- Create resentment and defensiveness
- Usurp the Holy Spirit's role in their life
- Damage intimacy (no one feels safe being vulnerable with someone constantly critiquing them)
- Focus on their shortcomings rather than your own (Matthew 7:3-5)

The Alternative: Accepting Without Enabling:

Acceptance doesn't mean:

- Ignoring sin or harmful behavior
- Never offering feedback or input
- Pretending problems don't exist
- Sacrificing your own needs completely

Acceptance does mean:

- Recognizing that personality differences are not moral failures
- Trusting that the Father will do His sanctifying work in His timing
- Focusing on your own growth rather than controlling theirs
- Loving them as God loves you – unconditionally "warts and all" while still desiring their growth
- Speaking truth when necessary, but with humility and love, not superiority

---

Key Principles to Remember:

1. You Are Not Your Spouse's Holy Spirit

Teaching: The Holy Spirit's Exclusive Role:

John 16:8 tells us the Holy Spirit's job: "And when He has come, He will convict the world of sin, and of righteousness, and of judgment." Notice that conviction is the Holy Spirit's work, not your work.

When you attempt to convict, correct, and change your spouse, you're trying to do the Holy Spirit's job. But you lack the Holy Spirit's qualifications:

- **Perfect knowledge**: The Holy Spirit knows your spouse's heart, motivations, and needs perfectly. You don't.
- **Perfect timing**: The Holy Spirit knows when to convict and when to extend grace. Your timing is often driven by your own frustrations.
- **Perfect love**: The Holy Spirit's conviction comes from pure love. Yours is often mixed with judgment, irritation, and self-interest.
- **Power to change**: The Holy Spirit can actually transform hearts. You cannot.

Your Role vs. The Spirit's Role:

- **The Spirit convicts**: You can gently speak truth when appropriate, but leave conviction to God
- **The Spirit sanctifies**: You can pray for their growth, but you can't manufacture it
- **The Spirit guides**: You can share perspective, but you can't force them to see things your way
- **The Spirit empowers change**: You can encourage, but only God gives power to truly change

Practical Application:

When you're frustrated with your spouse's personality trait or habit, ask yourself:

- Is this a sin issue or a preference issue?
- Am I trying to control or genuinely serve?
- Have I prayed about this more than I've nagged about it?
- How would I want to be approached if roles were reversed?
- Am I addressing this from love or irritation?

Individual Reflection:

1. What traits in your fiancé would you like to "fix" or change?

Be brutally honest in private reflection: What irritates you? What do you secretly hope will change after marriage? What have you already tried to adjust or influence? Is it their messiness? Their social needs? Their emotional expression? Their decision-making style? Their level of ambition? Their family involvement? Write these down—not to shame yourself, but to bring them into the light.

2. Why is it tempting to try to change someone we love?

Reflect deeply: What does your desire to change them reveal about you? Is it control? Insecurity? Genuine concern? Discomfort with differences? Unmet expectations? Where does this impulse come from? How have you felt when others have tried to change you?

---

3. How does God want to work in your life? In your fiancé's life?

Consider: What is God currently teaching you? Where do you need growth? What weaknesses has He revealed? Now think about your fiancé: What growth have you already witnessed in them? Where might God be working that you can't see? What if God's plan for their growth is different from yours?

---

2. Change Comes from God, Not Your Spouse

Teaching: How People Actually Change:

Human beings change through:

1. **Internal Conviction**: The Holy Spirit creates an internal desire for change. External pressure usually produces compliance or rebellion, not transformation.
2. **Safe Relationships**: People change in environments where they feel loved and accepted, not constantly criticized. Paradoxically, accepting your spouse as they are creates more space for growth than trying to change them.
3. **Divine Timing**: God works on His timeline, not yours. He may address the issue you're concerned about eventually, or He may be working on something more important first.
4. **Personal Responsibility**: Your spouse must take ownership of their growth/change. You can't want their growth/change more than they do.
5. **Grace and Truth**: Transformation happens when grace (acceptance, love, patience) and truth (honest feedback, accountability) work together (John 1:14).

The Prayer Approach:

Instead of nagging, trying to control, or manipulating, adopt a prayer-first approach:

- Pray about the issue more than you talk about it
- Ask God to reveal if this is truly a problem or just your preference
- Pray for your own patience and acceptance
- Ask God to work in their heart if change is needed
- Surrender control and trust God's work in them
- Finally: begin to praise Him for the change He is exacting in both of you

This doesn't mean you never discuss concerns - healthy marriages include honest conversation. But discussion should come from a place of prayer and trust in God's work, not from frustration and desire to control.

Discussion Together:

1. How can we encourage each other's growth without being controlling?

Establish guidelines for how you'll approach growth issues:

- **Timing**: When is the right time to offer feedback? (Not in public, not in the heat of anger, not when they're already stressed)
- **Tone**: What tone communicates love versus criticism?
- **Frequency**: How often is too often to bring up the same issue?
- **Invitation**: Ask permission: "Can I share an observation?" versus launching unsolicited critiques
- **Humility**: Acknowledge your own blind spots: "I may be wrong, but..."
- **Focus**: One issue at a time, not piling on multiple criticisms

---

2. What's the difference between helpful input and trying to change someone?

Discuss the line between healthy feedback and unhealthy control:

Helpful Input:

- Addresses specific behaviors, especially sin issues
- Is occasional and thoughtfully timed
- Comes from love and concern, not irritation
- Allows them to choose their response
- Is invited or welcomed (or at least not constantly resisted)
- Focuses on impact: "When you do X, I feel Y…"

Trying to Change Someone:

- Addresses personality traits or preferences
- Is constant and ongoing
- Comes from frustration or desire for control
- Demands they change to meet your needs
- Is unwelcome and creates defensiveness
- Focuses on judgment: "You shouldn't be this way"

---

3. How will we respond when we're frustrated with each other's personality differences?

Create a plan for moments of frustration:

- Take a break before speaking if you're angry
- Remind yourself this is personality, not defiance
- Pray before confronting
- Ask: "Is this worth addressing or should I extend grace?"
- Speak about your needs, not their failures: "I need…" versus "You always…"
- Appreciate their strengths even when frustrated with limitations
- Remember they're probably frustrated with your personality sometimes too

---

Part C: Celebrating How You're "Wired Together"

Teaching: From Tolerance to Celebration

Most couples move from attraction to tolerance regarding personality differences. Initially, differences are intriguing: "She's so spontaneous!" "He's so organized!" But familiarity breeds contempt, and soon those same traits irritate: "She's so irresponsible!" "He's so rigid!"

But God's design moves beyond mere tolerance to genuine celebration. Romans 12:10 instructs: "Be kindly affectionate to one another with brotherly love, in honor giving preference to one another." Notice the progression: affection, love, honor, preference. This isn't grudging acceptance—it's active appreciation.

Why Your Differences Are Good:

1. **Balance**: Your strengths compensate for each other's weaknesses. Where one is weak, the other is strong.
2. **Growth**: Your differences challenge you to expand beyond your comfort zone and develop new capacities. It's a joint adventure
3. **Perspective**: You see problems and opportunities from different angles, leading to better decisions.
4. **Team Effectiveness**: Different personalities handle different situations well. Together, you can handle more than either could alone.
5. **Sanctification**: Your differences reveal your selfishness, pride, and desire for control - driving you to grow in Christlikeness.
6. **Kingdom Impact**: Your combined gifts and personalities allow you to minister to more people than either of you could individually.

The Dance of Complementarity:

Think of your personalities like a dance. Two people doing the same moves at the same time create collision and redundancy. But complementary moves - one stepping forward while the other steps back, one spinning while the other provides stability - create beauty and effectiveness.

Your marriage works the same way. When you both try to lead, you clash. When you both withdraw, nothing moves forward. But when you embrace your different styles and move complementarily, you create something beautiful.

Personality Compatibility Assessment:

1. How do your personality styles complement each other?

Make a comprehensive list: Where does one person's strength cover the other's weakness? Examples: One is great with details while the other sees big picture;

one is calm in crisis while the other provides energy and optimism; one is socially skilled while the other provides depth in one-on-one relationships; one is decisive while the other is thoughtful. Celebrate these complementary patterns.

---

2. Where might your different styles create conflict?

Be realistic about friction points: Different communication styles (direct vs. indirect)? Different social needs (introvert vs. extrovert)? Different decision-making approaches (quick vs. deliberate)? Different organizational styles (structured vs. flexible)? Different emotional expression (reserved vs. expressive)? Identifying these now helps you prepare rather than being blindsided.

---

3. What can you learn to appreciate about your differences?

Shift perspective: Take each potential conflict area and find the positive side. Their "over-planning" is actually thoughtfulness and care. Your "spontaneity" is actually flexibility and adventure. Their "over-talking" is actually engagement and transparency. Your "quietness" is actually reflection and depth. Practice reframing differences as strengths rather than deficits.

---

4. How do your combined strengths make you a better team?

Think holistically: How does your marriage partnership allow you to accomplish, serve, and impact more than either of you could alone? How do your differences position you to minister to diverse people? How do you compensate for each other's blind spots? What becomes possible together that wasn't possible separately?

Practical Applications:

1. How will you handle decision-making given your different styles?

Create a decision-making framework that honors both styles:

- *If one needs to talk it through and the other needs to think quietly, build in both*
- *If one decides quickly and the other slowly, agree on timelines that accommodate both*
- *If one focuses on logic and the other on feelings, include both rational and emotional considerations*
- *If one sees opportunities and the other sees risks, value both optimism and caution*

---

2. What household responsibilities suit each of your personalities?

Divide tasks according to personality, not just gender stereotypes:

- *Who naturally notices when things need cleaning?*
- *Who enjoys cooking versus who finds it stressful?*
- *Who's better with financial details versus big-picture budgeting?*
- *Who's energized by social planning versus who finds it draining?*
- *Who prefers routine tasks versus variety?*

The goal is efficiency and reduced friction, not rigid equality in every category.

---

3. How can you support each other during stressful times?

Discuss stress responses:

- *When stressed, do you need space or connection?*
- *Do you need to talk it out or process internally?*
- *Do you need solutions or just empathy?*
- *Do you need encouragement or just silence?*
- *What support attempts feel helpful versus intrusive?*

Understanding these differences prevents the common pattern of one spouse withdrawing while the other pursues, each feeling unsupported.

4. What social situations energize or drain each of you?

Be specific about social needs:

- *How often do you each need social interaction?*
- *What size gatherings do you prefer (large parties vs. small dinners)?*
- *How long can you comfortably socialize before needing to recharge?*
- *What types of social activities energize versus exhaust you?*
- *How much alone time does each person need?*

Plan how you'll navigate these differences: attending events separately sometimes, arriving/leaving at different times, or alternating whose social preferences take priority.

Action Steps:

1. Create a "Personality Appreciation List" - write down what you love about your fiancé's personality

Each person should write a detailed list appreciating the other's personality traits:

- Their communication style
- Their emotional expression
- Their social tendencies
- Their decision-making approach
- Their organizational style
- Their stress response
- Their unique quirks

Be specific: Not just "I love that you're outgoing" but "I love how you make everyone feel welcome at gatherings, remember people's names, and create connection wherever you go."

Exchange lists and keep them accessible. When frustration arises, revisit this list to remember what you appreciate.

2. Identify potential conflict areas and discuss healthy ways to navigate them

For each identified conflict area, create a specific plan:

Example:

- **Conflict Area**: He needs quiet time after work; she wants to talk immediately
- **Healthy Navigation**: He gets 30 minutes alone when he arrives home, then they connect over dinner with full attention

Example:

- **Conflict Area**: She processes decisions by talking through options repeatedly; he finds this exhausting
- **Healthy Navigation**: She talks through decisions with friends/family first, then brings a narrowed list to him for final input

Write down your agreements so you can reference them later.

---

3. Plan how you'll remind each other of these insights when tensions arise

Create signals or phrases to de-escalate personality conflicts:

- "This is personality, not defiance" - reminder to both when friction occurs
- "Help me understand your perspective" - invitation to explain rather than defend
- "Can we revisit our personality discussion?" - suggestion to return to this chapter's insights
- "I'm frustrated, but I still appreciate you" - acknowledgment of both tension and commitment

Agree that either person can call a "personality timeout" when conflicts stem from temperament clashes rather than genuine issues requiring resolution.

Closing Reflection: Unity in Diversity

God could have made you and your fiancé identical. He didn't. Your personality differences are not obstacles to overcome but gifts to be enjoyed. The same Creator who delights in making billions of unique snowflakes and endless varieties of flora and fauna has designed you each uniquely - and then brought you together for purposes beyond your individual capacities.

The challenge before you is learning to appreciate rather than merely tolerate your differences, to celebrate rather than criticize the various ways God has wired your spouse together, and to trust that these differences are part of His good design for your marriage. When you stop trying to change each other and start working with each other's unique "blueprint", you'll discover the beauty of true partnership.

Remember: your spouse is not a project to fix but a person to love. The same grace God has extended to you - accepting you as you are while calling you to grow - is the grace you must extend to your spouse.

Prayer Suggestion:

"Father, thank You for creating [name] and [name] with such unique personalities. We praise You for the diversity of Your creation and for the specific ways You've wired each of us. Forgive us for the times we've tried to play Holy Spirit in each other's lives, attempting to change what only You can change. Help us to appreciate rather than criticize our differences. Give us patience with each other's limitations and gratitude for each other's strengths. Show us how our complementary personalities make us a more effective team for Your kingdom. When we're frustrated with personality differences, remind us that these differences are part of Your design. Help us move from tolerance to genuine celebration of how You've made us. May our unity in diversity reflect the Trinity's perfect unity. In Jesus' name, Amen."

Final Encouragement:

As you complete this chapter, you may feel both encouraged and concerned - encouraged by understanding, concerned about navigating differences. This is normal. Understanding personality is kind of like sanctification – it's a lifelong journey, not a one-time lesson. Be patient with yourselves and each other as you learn to dance together. The couple who masters the art of celebrating differences rather than criticizing them has discovered one of marriage's greatest secrets.

CHAPTER 6: GOD'S HEART FOR YOUR FINANCIAL WELL-BEING

Introduction: Money Matters to God

Few topics generate more anxiety, conflict, and disagreement in marriage than money. Financial stress is consistently cited as one of the leading causes of marital discord and divorce. Yet many couples avoid discussing finances until after the wedding, assuming love will somehow conquer all financial differences and challenges.

But being concerned with your future money matters is not merely practical – it's biblical. Jesus spoke about money more than almost any other topic, not because He was obsessed with finances, but because He understood that our relationship with money reveals our relationship with the Father. "For where your treasure is, there your heart will be also" (Matthew 6:21). How you earn, spend, save, give, and think about money reflects your deepest values, fears, and faith.

This chapter explores God's heart for your financial well-being - not as some term a "prosperity gospel that promises unlimited wealth without sacrifice," but as a biblical theology that recognizes God as a generous Father who desires to provide for His children while teaching them to steward His resources wisely for His kingdom purposes. You'll examine what Scripture actually teaches about prosperity, provision, and the relationship between spiritual health and financial blessing.

As you work through this material, approach it with humility and openness. Money touches on deeply held beliefs often inherited from family, cultural messages that may not be biblical, or personal experiences that shape how you view financial provision. Be willing to have your assumptions challenged by the Scriptures and recognize that building healthy financial habits as a couple begins with building a biblical theology of money.

Part A: Understanding Biblical Prosperity

Teaching: Defining True Prosperity

The Prosperity Debate:

The topic of prosperity theology creates strong reactions. Some Christians embrace an extreme "name it and claim it" prosperity gospel that equates faith with financial success and portrays God as a cosmic vending machine. Others react so strongly against these excesses that they adopt a poverty mentality, viewing wealth with suspicion and poverty as somehow being more spiritual than the rest.

The biblical position lies between what I see as extremes. Scripture neither promises universal wealth to all believers nor glorifies poverty as the ideal Christian state. Instead, it presents a nuanced view: God is a generous Provider who desires to bless His children, prosperity serves kingdom purposes beyond personal comfort, and both wealth and poverty come with spiritual dangers and responsibilities.

Defining True Prosperity: Read 3 John 1:2

"Beloved, I pray that you may prosper in all things and be in health, just as your soul prospers."

This brief verse reveals some very crucial truths:

1. **Prosperity is All-inclusive**: John's prayer encompasses "all things" - not just finances, but every dimension of life. True prosperity includes spiritual vitality, physical health, emotional well-being, relational richness, and yes, material provision.
2. **Prosperity is Progressive**: "Just as your soul prospers" suggests that different areas prosper at different rates. Your spiritual prosperity may outpace your financial prosperity, or vice versa. God's ultimate goal is wholeness in every area.
3. **Prosperity is Desired by God**: John prays this blessing because he knows it's God's will. This isn't a name-it-claim-it formula, but it does reveal God's heart - He's not opposed to His children prospering.
4. **Prosperity is Linked to Soul Health**: The connection between soul prosperity and overall prosperity is crucial. Your spiritual and emotional health directly impacts (and should impact) how you handle money, make financial decisions, and experience provision.

What Biblical Prosperity Is NOT:

- **Not guaranteed wealth for all believers**: Many faithful Christians live in "poverty" situations through no fault of their own, due to systemic injustice, geographic location, or persecution for their faith.
- **Not a right to demand from God**: We don't command God to bless us; we can walk in expectation of what He graciously has promised.
- **Not measured solely in money**: The wealthiest person may be impoverished spiritually. The materially poor may be the richest in faith (James 2:5).
- **Not an end in itself**: Biblical prosperity serves kingdom purposes - generosity, witness, and provision for ministry - not merely personal comfort.
- **Not divorced from obedience**: Financial blessing often follows faithful stewardship, hard work, and obedience to God's biblical principles.

What Biblical Prosperity IS:

- **God's desire for His children's well-being**: A loving Father wants His children to have what they need and even more - so they become His instruments of blessing to others.
- **Holistic flourishing**: Prosperity encompasses spiritual health, relational depth, purposeful work, and sufficient resources.
- **Stewardship opportunity**: Resources entrusted to us for wise management and kingdom purposes.
- **Tool for blessing others**: God blesses us to make us a blessing (Genesis 12:2).
- **Result of wise principles**: While not automatic, biblical financial principles generally lead to stability and increase.

Individual Reflection:

1. How do you define "prosperity"?

Before examining Scripture further, write your honest definition. Is it a certain income level? Freedom from debt? Ability to be generous? Security and stability? Luxury and comfort? Career success? Your definition reveals what you truly value and expect from God.

---

2. What messages about money did you receive growing up?

Reflect deeply on your family's financial culture: Was money abundant or scarce? Discussed openly or kept secret? A source of stress or security? Were you taught that wealthy people were greedy or that poverty was virtuous? Did your parents model generosity or lack thinking? Did they live within their means or constantly struggle with debt? These early messages profoundly shape your current money mindset, often unconsciously.

---

3. Do you believe God wants His children to prosper? Why or why not?

Examine your theology: Do you see God as a stingy Father who reluctantly provides the minimum, or as a generous Father who delights in blessing His children? Does your view come from Scripture or from your experience? Have you concluded that poverty is more spiritual, or that wealth indicates God's favor? What Bible passages have shaped your beliefs?

Biblical Foundation Study: Prosperity vs. Poverty - God's Original Design

Read Genesis 1:28-31 and 2:8-15

Before sin entered the world, God established His original design for humanity's relationship with provision and work:

God's Original Design (Pre-Fall):

1. **Abundance**: God placed Adam and Eve in a garden (literally "paradise") filled with everything they needed. Genesis 2:9 says God made "every tree grow that is pleasant to the sight and good for food." Beauty and provision were abundant.
2. **Work with Purpose**: Even in paradise, Adam worked - tending and keeping the garden (Genesis 2:15). Work was not a curse but a calling. It was fulfilling, fruitful, and unfrustrated.
3. **Fruitful Labor**: God blessed humanity with the command to "be fruitful and multiply" (Genesis 1:28). Their labor would produce results proportionate to their efforts.
4. **Dominion**: Humanity was given authority to "have dominion" over creation (Genesis 1:28). They were managers, not owners, stewarding God's creation for His glory.

5. **Generosity**: God freely gave "every herb that yields seed" and "every tree whose fruit yields seed" for food (Genesis 1:29). Provision was a gift, not something earned through toil and sweat.

This was God's design: meaningful work producing abundant fruit in a context of provision and blessing.

How the Fall Affected This Relationship (Read Genesis 3:17-19):

Sin didn't just affect humanity's relationship with God - it affected everything, including work and provision:

1. **Cursed Ground**: The earth itself was cursed, making work harder. "In toil you shall eat of it all the days of your life."
2. **Frustration**: Work became frustrating - "thorns and thistles" represent obstacles, setbacks, and unfruitful labor.
3. **Sweat and Struggle**: Provision now required "the sweat of your face." Labor became toilsome rather than joyful.
4. **Return to Dust**: Death entered, bringing ultimate loss and the reality that we can't take earthly wealth with us.

The fall introduced poverty, lack, frustration in work, and the curse of scarcity. But this was not God's original design, and through Christ, redemption would come.

Key Scripture Study Together: Read Galatians 3:13-14

"Christ has redeemed us from the curse of the law, having become a curse for us (for it is written, 'Cursed is everyone who hangs on a tree'), that the blessing of Abraham might come upon the Gentiles in Christ Jesus, that we might receive the promise of the Spirit through faith."

Critical Questions for Discussion:

1. How has Christ redeemed us from the curse of poverty?

Discuss together: Galatians 3:13 says Christ redeemed us from "the curse of the law." Deuteronomy 28 details the blessings of obedience (including material provision—verses 1-14) and curses of disobedience (including poverty, lack, and failure—verses 15-68).

The curse included financial dimensions: debt, crop failure, poverty, and economic oppression. Christ's redemption on the cross doesn't automatically make every Christian wealthy, but it does break the spiritual curse of poverty over those who trust Him. We're no longer under the curse - we're positioned for blessing.

This doesn't mean poverty never touches Christians, but it does mean:

- We have access to God's provision through faith
- We're no longer spiritually cursed with perpetual lack
- God's heart toward us is blessing, not cursing
- We can expect Him to provide for our needs
- Faithful stewardship often leads to increase

---

2. What does it mean that "the blessing of Abraham might come upon the Gentiles"?

Study together what the blessing of Abraham included:

- Genesis 12:2-3: God would make Abraham's name great and make him a blessing
- Genesis 13:2: Abraham became "very rich in livestock, in silver, and in gold"
- Genesis 24:35: "The Lord has blessed my master greatly, and he has become great"

The blessing wasn't just spiritual - it included material provision. But notice the purpose: Abraham was blessed to be a blessing. God told him, "I will bless you...and you shall be a blessing...and in you all the families of the earth shall be blessed" (Genesis 12:2-3).

As spiritual children of Abraham through faith in Christ (Galatians 3:29), we inherit this blessing - not for selfish accumulation, but to extend blessing to others. We're blessed to be generous, blessed to advance God's kingdom, blessed to provide for our families and to bless our communities.

Part B: God as Our Source

Teaching: Every Good Gift Comes from Above

Read James 1:17

"Every good gift and every perfect gift is from above, and comes down from the Father of lights, with whom there is no variation or shadow of turning."

God as Source vs. Your Job as Source:

One of the most important financial mindset shifts is recognizing God as your ultimate source, not your employer, clients, investments, or even your own skills. Your job is a channel through which God provides, but He is the source.

Why does this distinction matter?

1. **During Job Loss**: If you view your job as your source, losing it creates panic and crisis of faith. If you view God as your source, you trust He'll provide through another channel.
2. **In Career Decisions**: When you know God is your source, you can make decisions based on calling rather than only money. You're free to follow God's leading even when it doesn't make financial sense from a human perspective.
3. **In Generosity**: When you see God as your source, tithes and offerings do not deplete you - you're simply redistributing what He's already provided and trusting Him to provide more.
4. **In Times of Abundance**: When you prosper, you don't credit yourself or your job - you thank God as you steward His blessings wisely.
5. **In Anxiety**: When financial stress hits, you pray to your Source rather than merely scrambling for solutions in your own strength.

Practical Application:

This isn't passive resignation ("I'll just wait for God to drop money from heaven"). God typically provides through:

- Employment and hard work (2 Thessalonians 3:10)
- Wise stewardship and planning (Proverbs 21:5)
- Creative solutions and opportunities He furnishes
- Unexpected provisions that only He could orchestrate
- The generosity of others responding to His leading

You work diligently while trusting ultimately in God's provision, not your own efforts.

Abraham's Covenant - Our Example:

Study Together:

Genesis 26:12-14 (Isaac's Prosperity):

"Then Isaac sowed in that land and reaped in the same year a hundredfold; and the Lord blessed him. The man began to prosper and continued prospering until he became very prosperous; for he had possessions of flocks and possessions of herds and a great number of servants. So, the Philistines envied him."

Notice the pattern:

1. Isaac sowed (he worked)
2. He reaped a hundredfold (supernatural multiplication)
3. The Lord blessed him (divine favor acknowledged)
4. He continued prospering (progressive increase)
5. Others envied him (his prosperity was noticeable)

Genesis 30:43 (Jacob's Increase):

"Thus, the man became exceedingly prosperous, and had large flocks, female and male servants, and camels and donkeys."

Again, progressive prosperity that was noticeable and attributed to God's blessing.

Proverbs 10:22:

"The blessing of the Lord makes one rich, and He adds no sorrow with it."

This verse distinguishes between wealth gained through godly means versus ungodly means:

- Godly prosperity comes with peace, not anxiety
- God's blessing doesn't require compromising integrity
- True prosperity brings joy, not the sorrow of broken relationships, guilty conscience, or slavery to money

Key Observations:

These patriarchs weren't just spiritually blessed. Their wealth:

- Came from God's blessing on their labor
- Enabled them to fulfill God's purposes
- Made them witnesses to surrounding nations
- Positioned them to be generous
- Didn't compromise their relationship with God

Discussion Questions:

1. How does knowing God as your source change your approach to finances?

Discuss practical implications:

- How does it affect career decisions when you know God is your provider?
- How does it impact giving when you trust God's supply?
- How does it reduce financial anxiety?
- How does it change how you handle setbacks or unexpected expenses?
- How does it affect your prayers about finances?

---

2. What promises did God make to Abraham that apply to us today?

Review the Abrahamic covenant (Genesis 12, 15, 17) and discuss which promises apply to Christians as spiritual children of Abraham:

- Blessing (Genesis 12:2)
- Being made a blessing to others (Genesis 12:2)
- Protection (Genesis 12:3)
- Numerous descendants—spiritual children through faith (Genesis 15:5)
- Covenant relationship with God (Genesis 17:7)

Which of these promises give you confidence about God's provision in your marriage?

3. How does prosperity enable us to fulfill God's purposes?

Brainstorm together:

- How does financial stability free you to serve in ministry?
- How does generosity require resources?
- How does provision allow you to be hospitable?
- How does financial margin create space for opportunities (missions trips, helping others in need, supporting causes)?
- How could prosperity in your marriage advance God's kingdom?

Part C: Jesus and the Better Covenant

Teaching: The New Covenant's Better Promises

Read Hebrews 8:6 together:

"But now He has obtained a more excellent ministry, inasmuch as He is also Mediator of a better covenant, which was established on better promises."

The Old vs. New Covenant:

The Old Covenant (Mosaic Law) promised blessings for obedience and curses for disobedience (Deuteronomy 28). But it required perfect obedience, which no one could achieve. The law revealed sin but couldn't provide power to overcome it.

The New Covenant, established through Christ's atoning work at the cross, is superior because:

1. **It is Based on Grace, Not Works**: We receive blessing not by perfect obedience but by faith in Christ's perfect obedience (Ephesians 2:8-9).
2. **It is Permanent, Not Conditional**: Our standing before God doesn't fluctuate based on our performance. Christ secured our position permanently.
3. **It is an Internal Transformation**: The Holy Spirit writes God's law on our hearts, giving us power to obey from love rather than mere duty (Hebrews 8:10).
4. **It is Complete Forgiveness**: "I will be merciful to their unrighteousness, and their sins and their lawless deeds I will remember no more" (Hebrews 8:12).

Read Galatians 3:26-29:

"For you are all sons of God through faith in Christ Jesus. For as many of you as were baptized into Christ have put on Christ. There is neither Jew nor Greek, there is neither slave nor free, there is neither male nor female; for you are all one in Christ Jesus. And if you are Christ's, then you are Abraham's seed, and heirs according to the promise."

You Are Abraham's Seed:

Through faith in Christ, Gentile believers are grafted into Abraham's family tree. We're not second-class citizens in God's kingdom - we're full heirs of the Abrahamic covenant and promises. This includes:

- Blessing in every area of life
- Positioned to be a blessing to others
- God's faithfulness to provide
- Covenant relationship with the God who owns everything

This doesn't mean you can claim Abraham's specific wealth, but it does mean you have access to the same God who provided for Abraham and the same covenant relationship of blessing.

God's Desire for Your Completeness:

Study 1 Thessalonians 5:23 and 3 John 1:2:

"Now may the God of peace Himself sanctify you completely; and may your whole spirit, soul, and body be preserved blameless at the coming of our Lord Jesus Christ." (1 Thessalonians 5.23)

"Beloved, I pray that you may prosper in all things and be in health, just as your soul prospers." (3 John 1:2)

Discussion Questions:

1. How does God want you to prosper in spirit, soul, and body?

Discuss holistic prosperity:

- **Spirit**: Growing relationship with God, spiritual vitality, fruitfulness in ministry
- **Soul**: Emotional health, mental clarity, purposeful life, healthy relationships
- **Body**: Physical health, energy, provision for physical needs (food, shelter, clothing)

God doesn't compartmentalize. He desires your wholeness - your spiritual prosperity supporting your emotional health, which enables physical well-being, which provides stability for continued spiritual growth.

---

2. What role does financial provision play in your overall well-being?

Be honest about money's role:

- Financial stress affects physical health (stress-related illness)
- Money problems create emotional anxiety and relational strains
- Financial stability creates margin for spiritual growth (less consumed by survival)
- Provision enables you to be generous, which brings joy
- Lack of basic needs makes it difficult to focus on higher purposes

Money isn't everything but pretending it doesn't matter spiritually is naive. Financial provision is one component of God's complete care for you.

Part D: Living Without Lack

Teaching: God's Provision Promises

Read Together:

James 1:3-4: "Knowing that the testing of your faith produces patience. But let patience have its perfect work, that you may be perfect and complete, lacking nothing."

2 Corinthians 9:8: "And God is able to make all grace abound toward you, that you, always having all sufficiency in all things, may have an abundance for every good work."

Philippians 4:19: "And my God shall supply all your needs according to His riches in glory by Christ Jesus."

The Promise of "Lacking Nothing":

These verses paint a picture of God's provision that's comprehensive and sufficient. But we must understand what they promise and what they don't:

What These Verses Promise:

- God will provide what we genuinely need
- His provision will be sufficient for His purposes in our lives
- We'll have enough not just for ourselves, but for "every good work"
- His resources (heaven's riches) are the measure, not man's earthly economy
- Faith-testing produces patience that leads to spiritual completeness

What These Verses Don't Promise:

- You'll have everything you want
- You'll never experience financial pressure or testing
- You won't need to work or exercise wisdom
- You'll be wealthy by worldly standards
- Provision will always come on your preferred timeline

The Context of Philippians 4:19:

It's crucial to read Philippians 4:19 in context. Paul writes this immediately after thanking the Philippians for their financial partnership in ministry (Philippians 4:14-18). They gave sacrificially to support Paul's missionary work, and he assures them that God will supply their needs in return.

This connects giving and receiving - those who invest in kingdom work can trust God's provision. It's not a blank check for selfish consumption, but a promise for those partnering with God's purposes. It is a wonderful example of the biblical principle of seedtime and harvest.

Couple Discussion:

1. What does "lacking nothing" mean practically in marriage?

Discuss realistic expectations:

- Does it mean never experiencing financial stress?
- Does it mean always having money for everything you'd like to do?
- Does it mean trusting God will provide what you actually need, when you need it?
- How do you distinguish between needs and wants?
- What "lack" would you find most difficult to trust God through?

---

2. How can we trust God's provision during uncertain times?

Create practical strategies for building trust:

- Regular prayer, especially thanksgiving, about finances, not just in crisis
- Journaling God's past provision to remember His faithfulness
- Building emergency savings as stewardship, not lack of faith – its building our "storehouse".
- Supporting each other's faith when one struggles with anxiety
- Seeking godly counsel during financial decisions
- Practicing generosity even in lean seasons
- Remembering biblical examples of God's provision (ravens feeding Elijah, manna in wilderness, widow's oil, etc.)

---

3. What does it mean to "always have all sufficiency in all things"? (2 Corinthians 9:8)

Unpack this comprehensive promise:

- "Always" = in every season, not just abundance
- "All sufficiency" = enough, not necessarily excess
- "In all things" = every area, not just money
- Purpose: "abundance for every good work" = provision enables ministry

This is promise of adequacy for God's purposes, not unlimited wealth for personal consumption.

Deuteronomy 8:18 - Covenant Relationships:

"And you shall remember the Lord your God, for it is He who gives you power to get wealth, that He may establish His covenant which He swore to your fathers, as it is this day."

Teaching: The Power to Obtain Wealth:

This verse reveals several crucial truths:

1. God Gives Power to Obtain Wealth

God doesn't usually rain money from heaven. Instead, He gives:

- Skills and abilities
- Intelligence and creativity
- Opportunities and favor
- Strength to work
- Wisdom for decisions
- Connections with people
- Ideas and innovation

Your capacity to earn comes from God. Even your work ethic, discipline, and intelligence are gifts from Him.

2. The Purpose of Prosperity: "That He May Establish His Covenant"

Wealth serves covenant purposes:

- Demonstrating God's faithfulness to His promises
- Enabling you to fulfill His purposes
- Positioning you to bless others
- Providing resources for kingdom advancement
- Being a witness to unbelievers of God's goodness

When prosperity serves these purposes rather than selfish accumulation, it aligns with God's heart.

Discussion Questions:

1. How does God give us power to obtain wealth?

Identify specific ways God has equipped you:

* What skills, education, or abilities has He given you?
* What opportunities has He opened?
* What favor have you experienced?
* How has He provided beyond your own efforts?
* What strengths do you each bring to your financial partnership?

---

2. What is the purpose of this prosperity?

Discuss together:

* How does prosperity "establish His covenant"?
* What kingdom purposes could financial increase serve in your marriage?
* How can you ensure wealth serves God's purposes, not just comfort?
* What would it look like to steward prosperity as covenant partners with God?

Part E: Applying These Truths to Your Marriage

Teaching: From Theology to Practice

Understanding God's heart for financial well-being is foundational, but it must translate into practical decisions, habits, and attitudes in your marriage. Biblical prosperity was never about receiving. It was always about becoming the kind of people who can be trusted with resources, who use wealth wisely, and who advance God's Kingdom through faithful stewardship.

Key Principles for Application:

1. Renew Your Mind About Money

Romans 12:2 calls us to be "transformed by the renewing of your mind." Many Christians hold unbiblical beliefs about money and so they limit God's work:

* "Money is the root of all evil" (No; the _love_ of money is evil, 1 Timothy 6:10)
* "Poverty is more spiritual" (No; both wealth and poverty have spiritual dangers)
* "God doesn't care about my finances" (No; He cares about every detail of your life)

- "I can't trust God with <u>my</u> money" (No; He's proven trustworthy throughout history)

Identify limiting beliefs and replace them with biblical truth.

2. Position Yourself for Blessing

While you can't manipulate God, you can position yourself to receive:

- **Obedience**: "If you are willing and obedient, you shall eat the good of the land" (Isaiah 1:19)
- **Generosity**: "Give, and it will be given to you" (Luke 6:38)
- **Diligence**: "The hand of the diligent makes rich" (Proverbs 10:4)
- **Wisdom**: "Through wisdom a house is built, and by understanding it is established; by knowledge the rooms are filled with all precious and pleasant riches" (Proverbs 24:3-4)
- **Integrity**: "Better is the poor who walks in his integrity than one perverse in his ways, though he be rich" (Proverbs 28:6)

3. Steward Faithfully What You Have

Don't despise small beginnings or wait until you have "enough" to be faithful. Jesus' parable of the talents (Matthew 25:14-30) shows that faithfulness with little leads to increase. Steward well what God has already given:

- Budget wisely
- Avoid unnecessary debt
- Save consistently
- Give generously from whatever level you're at
- Work diligently
- Make wise decisions

4. Keep Prosperity in Perspective

Never make wealth your goal or your identity. Paul warns: "Command those who are rich in this present age not to be haughty, nor to trust in uncertain riches but in the living God, who gives us richly all things to enjoy" (1 Timothy 6:17).

<u>Prosperity is a tool, not a trophy</u>. It's a means to kingdom ends, not an end in itself. Hold wealth with an open hand, ready to give as God directs.

Personal Application: (Talk it Over)

1. How will understanding God's heart for prosperity affect your financial decisions?

Be specific about changes you anticipate: Will you be more generous? Less anxious? More strategic in career? More willing to trust God with risks? More faithful in stewardship? How will this teaching change how you think about saving, spending, giving, and earning?

2. What limiting beliefs about money do you need to surrender to God?

Identify specific beliefs that don't align with Scripture: Do you believe you'll never have enough? That wealthy people are greedy? That you don't deserve prosperity? That it's too late for you financially? That God won't provide? Write these down, confess them, and replace them with biblical truth.

3. How can you encourage each other to receive from God's abundance?

Discuss practical ways to build faith together: Will you share testimonies of provision? Pray specifically about finances? Remind each other of God's promises during tight seasons? Celebrate when God provides? Challenge scarcity thinking in each other? How will you create a culture of faith rather than fear around money?

Action Steps:

1. Pray together, thanking God for His desire to bless you

Set aside time for focused prayer. Thank God specifically for:

- His generous nature as your heavenly Father
- The provision He's already supplied in your lives
- The redemption from the curse through Christ
- Your identity as children of Abraham by faith
- The covenant promises that apply to you
- The power He gives you to obtain wealth

- His faithfulness to provide for all your needs
- The privilege of being blessed to be a blessing

---

2. Identify any poverty mindsets that need to be replaced with God's Word

Make a list of poverty mindsets you've identified (from family, culture, or experience):

Example:

- Poverty Mindset: "There's never enough"
- Biblical Truth: "My God shall supply all your need" (Philippians 4:19)

Example:

- Poverty Mindset: "Rich people are greedy"
- Biblical Truth: "The blessing of the Lord makes rich, and adds no sorrow" (Proverbs 10:22)

Example:

- Poverty Mindset: "I don't deserve to prosper"
- Biblical Truth: "Christ redeemed us from the curse" (Galatians 3:13)

For each poverty mindset, find a Scripture to replace it with truth. Memorize these verses and speak them when scarcity thinking arises.

---

3. Discuss how you want to steward God's blessings as a married couple

Have a vision-casting conversation:

- How do you want to handle finances in your marriage? (Covered more in next chapter, but begin thinking here)
- What percentage do you want to give to God's work?
- How will you balance saving and generosity?
- What financial goals align with your kingdom values?
- How can your financial partnership display God's faithfulness?
- What would it look like to be "blessed to be a blessing" practically?
- If God prospered you beyond your needs, how would you steward it?

Closing Reflection: Prosperity with Purpose

God's heart for your financial well-being is not about making you rich for your own sake. It's about establishing His covenant, demonstrating His faithfulness, equipping you for the Kingdom work, and positioning you to be generous conduits of His blessing to others.

As you prepare for marriage, build your financial foundation on these truths: God is your source, He desires to bless you, His provision is sufficient for His purposes in your life, and prosperity serves kingdom purposes beyond personal comfort. When you align your financial life with these principles - working diligently, stewarding faithfully, giving generously, and trusting faithfully - you position yourselves to experience God's provision and become His source of blessing to others.

Remember that prosperity is not measured only in bank accounts but in ones complete well-being: spirit, soul, and body. The couple who prospers in all three dimensions and uses their resources to advance God's Kingdom has discovered the secret of biblical prosperity.

Prayer Suggestion:

"Father, thank You for being our generous Provider and the source of every good gift. We reject poverty mindsets that limit Your work in our lives, and we embrace Your heart for our prosperity. We receive by faith the blessings of Abraham that comes to us through Christ. Give us power to obtain wealth, not for selfish purposes, but to establish Your covenant and advance Your Kingdom. Help us to be faithful stewards of whatever You provide, whether little or much. Teach us to work diligently, give generously, save wisely, and trust completely in Your provision. May our financial life as a married couple display Your faithfulness and draw others to You. We commit our finances to You, trusting that as we seek first Your Kingdom, all these things will be added to us. In Jesus' name, Amen."

Final Note:

This chapter established the theological foundation for biblical prosperity. The next chapter will address practical financial management - budgeting, debt, giving, and financial decision-making as a couple. Understanding God's heart (this chapter) must precede practical application (next chapter), because your theology drives your methodology. If you're unclear about anything in this chapter or if you and your fiancé hold significantly different views on prosperity theology, discuss these differences now with your facilitator before proceeding to practical financial planning.

CHAPTER 7: FAITHFUL STEWARDSHIP THROUGH TITHING

Introduction: The First Tenth

Of all the financial topics couples must navigate, few generate more debate, confusion, and strong opinions than Tithing and Offerings. Some Christians consider the Tithe a non-negotiable biblical command that applies to all believers in all times. Others view it as an Old Testament practice fulfilled in Christ, replaced by grace-motivated giving without percentage requirements. Still others practice Tithing but struggle with questions: Should we tithe on gross or net income? Does it all go to the local church, or can we tithe to some other ministries? What if we genuinely can't afford to tithe right now?

These aren't just theological questions, they're deeply practical issues that will affect your marriage's financial health, spiritual vitality, relationship with God and possibly with each other. How you handle money reveals what you truly believe about God's ownership, His provision, and His trustworthiness. Jesus said, "Where your treasure is, there your heart will be also" (Matthew 6:21). In many instances your giving patterns are a spiritual barometer, measuring the temperature of your faith.

This chapter explores the biblical foundation for tithes and offerings, tracing them from before the Law through the New Testament era and on into today. You'll examine where the tithe should be given, why it matters, and how to implement faithful stewardship as a married couple. You'll also address common objections, challenges, and questions about tithes and offerings in the context of grace.

As you work through this material, approach it with humility and openness. For instance, if you've never tithed before, this teaching may challenge you to take a significant step of faith. If you've tithed faithfully for years, this chapter may deepen your understanding of why tithes and offerings matter and help you establish unity with your future spouse. Most importantly, this chapter is about more than money - it's about lordship, trust, and positioning yourselves to receive God's blessing in your marriage.

Part A: Understanding the Tithe

Teaching: Defining the Tithe

Biblical Definition: Read Leviticus 27:30

"And all the tithe of the land, whether of the seed of the land or of the fruit of the tree, is the Lord's. It is holy to the Lord."

This verse establishes several foundational truths about the tithe:

1. The Tithe Belongs to God: "It is the Lord's"

This is crucial: the tithe isn't your money that you give to God. It's His money that you return to Him. You don't own the tithe, so you can't "give" your tithe. You're merely the delivery person. When you keep the tithe, you're not being stingy with your money; you're keeping what belongs to the Lord.

Think of it this way: if your employer pays you for 40 hours of work but you only worked 36, you've stolen from your employer. Similarly, if God entrusts you with income and you keep the portion that belongs to Him, you've taken what isn't yours. Malachi 3:8 makes this explicit: "Will a man rob God? Yet you have robbed Me! But you say, 'In what way have we robbed You?' In tithes and offerings."

And one last note. You can not "give" your tithe. You can "give" your offerings, but you can't "give" your tithe. The tithe belongs to the Lord, you can only "bring" your tithe. You can't "give" what you don't own.

2. The Tithe is Holy: "It is holy to the Lord"

"Holy" means "set apart," "consecrated for sacred use." The tithe isn't ordinary money. The tithe is sacred money designated for God's purposes. Treating it as common funds for personal use violates its holy status.

This is why tithing from leftovers rather than first fruits is problematic. When you pay all your bills, enjoy entertainment, and then give God whatever remains, you've treated His portion as less important than your own expenses. But when you honor the tithe as holy, you give it priority. It's first, not last.

3. The Tithe is Ten Percent: "all the tithe"

While the word "tithe" literally means "tenth," the specific percentage matters because it represents:

- **Equality**: The person tithing on $30,000 brings $3,000; the wealthy person tithing on $300,000 brings $30,000. The percentage is the same, though the amounts differ dramatically. God's system is proportional, not flat.
- **Measurability**: Ten percent provides a clear, objective standard. You know whether you've tithed or not.
- **Significant but Not Crushing**: Ten percent is substantial enough to require faith but not so large that it's impossible.

What is the Tithe?

Let's clarify what the tithe actually is:

1. The tithe is one-tenth (10%) of your income

This is straightforward: whatever income you receive, 10% is the tithe. If you earn $4,000 per month, your tithe is $400. If you receive $10,000 annually, your tithe is $1,000.

2. It comes from your gross income, not what's left over after expenses

This is where many Christians struggle. Should you tithe on a gross income (before taxes and deductions) or net income (what you actually receive)?

Biblical principle: First fruits, not leftovers.

Proverbs 3:9 says, "Honor the Lord with your possessions, and with the first fruits of all your increase." First fruits means the first portion, not what's left after everyone else gets their portion.

When the Israelites brought their harvest to God, they didn't pay the tax collector first, settle their debts first, and then give God the remainder. They gave Him the first and the best.

Practically, this means tithing on your gross income. If your paycheck shows $5,000 gross with $1,000 in taxes and deductions, resulting in $4,000 net pay, your tithe should be $500 (10% of $5,000), not $400 (10% of $4,000).

Some argue, "But I never see that tax money! Why should I tithe on it?" Because God blessed you with the job that produces that gross income. The taxes are part of your stewardship responsibility ("Render to Caesar the things that are Caesar's" - Mark 12:17), but they don't negate your responsibility to bring God His portion first.

3. It represents bringing to God the "first fruits" of your increase

First fruits means:

- **Priority**: God gets His portion before you pay bills, before you buy groceries, before you buy that new phone, before anything else
- **Trust**: Giving first fruits requires faith that God will provide
- **Honor**: First fruits demonstrates that God is most important, not least important

4. It's not leftovers, but a priority in acknowledging God as our source

When you tithe from first fruits, you're making a declaration: "God, You are my source. You provided this income, and I trust You to provide for all my needs."

This is radically countercultural. The world's wisdom says: "Pay your bills first, then give from what's left." God's wisdom says: "Honor Me first, and I'll take care of everything else."

Individual Reflection:

1. How do you currently view tithing?

Be completely honest: Do you see tithing as legalism, obedience, opportunity, burden, Old Testament requirement, New Testament principle, or something else? Do you currently tithe? If so, consistently or sporadically? On gross or net? If not, why not? What emotions does the topic of tithing evoke in you? Guilt?, Joy?, Confusion?, Resistance?

---

2. What questions or concerns do you have about tithing?

Write down every question without filtering: Can I afford it? Is it still required under grace? What if my spouse doesn't agree? Where should it go? What about student loans and debt? Is it legalistic? What if I can't pay my bills if I tithe? Do I tithe on gifts and tax refunds? These questions are valid, identifying them is the first step toward finding biblical answers.

---

3. How were you taught about giving in your family growing up?

Reflect on your family's giving culture: Did your parents tithe faithfully? Was money tight, and giving seemed impossible? Did you see generous giving modeled? Was financial giving discussed openly or kept private? Did your family trust God with finances, or was there chronic anxiety about money? These early experiences profoundly shape your current attitudes toward tithing.

Part B: The Tithe - Older Than the Law

Teaching: Tithing Before Moses

One common objection to tithing goes like this: "Tithing was part of the Old Testament Law given to Israel. Christians aren't under the Law, we're under grace. Therefore, tithing doesn't apply to us."

This argument has a fatal flaw: tithing predates the Mosaic Law by over four centuries. The tithe wasn't invented at Mount Sinai! It was practiced long before and simply incorporated into the Law. If tithing were merely a legal requirement fulfilled in Christ, we'd expect to see it introduced for the first time in Exodus, Leviticus, or Deuteronomy. Instead, we find it practiced by the patriarchs generations earlier.

Historical Foundation: Study Together

Genesis 14:17-20 (Abraham brings his tithes to Melchizedek):

"And the king of Sodom went out to meet him at the Valley of Shaveh (that is, the King's Valley), after his return from the defeat of Chedorlaomer and the kings who were with him. Then Melchizedek king of Salem brought out bread and wine; he was the priest of God Most High. And he (Melchizedek) blessed him (Abram) and said: 'Blessed be Abram of God Most High, Possessor of heaven and earth; and blessed be God Most High, who has delivered your enemies into your hand.' And he (Abram) gave him (Melchizedek) a tithe of all."

Context: Abraham had just defeated a coalition of kings to rescue his nephew Lot. He recovered all the goods that had been taken. On his return, he encountered Melchizedek, a mysterious figure described as "priest of God Most High." In response to Melchizedek's blessing, Abraham tithed to him of all he had recovered.

Key Observations:

1. **This occurred around 2000 BC, roughly 430 years before the Law was given** (Galatians 3:17). Tithing clearly predates the Mosaic covenant.
2. **Abram tithed voluntarily, not under legal compulsion.** No law commanded it; he did it from the heart, recognizing God as the source of his victory.
3. **Abram tithed to a priest who represented God.** This establishes the pattern of bringing the tithe to God's representative, not just giving it anywhere.
4. **The tithe represented worship and recognition of God's provision.** Abram's tithe was an act of thanksgiving and acknowledgment that his victory came from the Lord.

Hebrews 7:1-9 (The significance of Abraham's tithe):

The New Testament Commentary on Abraham's Tithe:

The book of Hebrews, written to Christians under the New Covenant, uses Abraham's tithe to make theological points:

1. **Melchizedek was greater than Abraham** because he received tithes from the patriarch and blessed him. The one who blesses is greater than the one blessed.
2. **The Levitical priesthood was inferior to Melchizedek's priesthood** because even Levi (who hadn't been born yet) paid tithes to Melchizedek "through Abraham."
3. **Christ's priesthood follows Melchizedek's order, not Levi's** (Hebrews 7:11-17). Jesus is our High Priest in the order of Melchizedek.

The Implication for Christians:

If tithing was only a Levitical requirement, and Christ's priesthood replaces the Levitical priesthood, one might argue we don't tithe anymore. But Hebrews makes the opposite argument: Because Christ's priesthood follows Melchizedek's order (not Levi's), and because Abraham tithed to Melchizedek centuries before the Law, tithing is actually more fundamental than the Law - it's a patriarchal practice rooted in faith and relationship with God.

The Levitical tithe was a legal requirement for Israel under the Old Covenant. The patriarchal tithe (Abraham's model) was a voluntary act of worship and faith. Christians aren't obligated to follow the Levitical system, but Abraham's example of faith-based giving remains instructive for all who are his spiritual children (Galatians 3:7: "Therefore know that only those who are of faith are sons of Abraham").

Key Points to Discuss:

1. The tithe was established 430 years before the Mosaic Law

2. It's based on relationship with God, not legal obligation

3. Abraham tithed by faith, recognizing God as his provider

Couple Discussion:

1. How does knowing tithing predates the Law affect your view of it?

Discuss how this changes the common objection that "tithing is Old Testament Law." Does knowing Abraham tithed voluntarily by faith make tithing more appealing or compelling? How does this historical context affect your willingness to adopt tithing as a practice in your marriage?

---

2. What does Abraham's example teach us about giving?

Identify principles from Abraham's tithe:

- He gave from gratitude for God's provision (victory in battle)
- He gave voluntarily, not under compulsion
- He gave to God's representative (priest)
- He gave proportionally (tenth of all)
- He gave as an act of worship

Which of these principles resonates most with you? How can you apply them?

Part C: Where Should We Give Our Tithe?

Teaching: The Destination of the Tithe

Understanding what the tithe is and why we give it is important, but practical questions remain: Where does the tithe go? Can we split it between multiple ministries? What if we want to support missionaries, the poor, or other causes - does that count as our tithe?

To Whom Are We Giving? Read Hebrews 7:8

"Here mortal men receive tithes, but there he receives them, of whom it is witnessed that he lives."

This verse contains a crucial insight: while human ministers receive tithes physically, ultimately Jesus receives them. When you write a check to your church, you're not just supporting an organization -you're giving to Christ through His representatives.

This transforms how we view tithing. It's not merely a financial transaction or church membership obligation - it's an act of worship directed toward Christ Himself.

Old Testament Pattern: Study Together

Deuteronomy 26:1-4 (Bringing first fruits to the priest):

Key Pattern: First fruits were brought to the priest at the designated place of worship - the tabernacle, and later the temple. This wasn't a casual distribution to various causes; it was a formal presentation at God's dwelling place through His appointed ministers.

Numbers 18:21-26 (Tithes given to the Levites):

Key Pattern: The tithe supported those who ministered full-time in God's house. The Levites had no land inheritance - they depended on the tithes. Interestingly, the Levites then tithed on what they received (a tithe of the tithe), demonstrating that even those receiving tithes were required to give.

Nehemiah 10:37-39 (Tithes brought to the house of God):

Key Pattern: Tithes were brought to "the house of our God" - the central place of worship, not distributed individually to various causes. This "storehouse" concept becomes important in Malachi 3:10.

New Testament Application:

Principle 1: We bring our tithe to the Lord through His representatives

Just as the Israelites brought tithes to the priests, Christians bring tithes to those who minister spiritually. These are primarily pastors and church leaders. First Timothy 5:17-18 says: "Let the elders who rule well be counted worthy of double honor, especially those who labor in the word and doctrine. For the Scripture says, 'You shall not muzzle an ox while it treads out the grain,' and, 'The laborer is worthy of his wages.'" Paul is connecting pastoral ministry to the Old Testament provision for priests.

Principle 2: The local church is typically the "storehouse" for today's believers

Malachi 3:10 says, "Bring all the tithes into the storehouse, that there may be food in My house." The "storehouse" was the temple - the central place of worship and ministry. For Christians, the local church functions as the storehouse. This is where:

- You receive spiritual feeding through teaching and worship
- You're part of a covenant community
- Pastoral care and oversight function
- Ministry happens that requires financial support

Principle 3: Pastoral ministry corresponds to the Levitical priesthood

While all believers are part of a "royal priesthood" (1 Peter 2:9), there remains a distinct pastoral office that corresponds functionally to the Levitical priesthood. Pastors are set apart for full-time ministry, depend on the financial support of those they serve, and represent God's interests to the people. Your tithe supports this vital ministry.

What About Supporting Other Ministries?

This is where offerings come in (discussed in Part E). The tithe goes to your local church leadership - the spiritual house where you're fed and serve. Support for missionaries, parachurch organizations, Christian schools, the poor, and other worthy causes comes from our offerings which are above and beyond the tithe, not by redirecting the tithe away from the local church.

Some argue, "But my church is wealthy and doesn't need my tithe. Shouldn't I give it where there's greater need?" This reasoning, while seemingly compassionate, misses the point. Tithing isn't about the church's neediness. Tithing is about your obedience and the principle of bringing the tithe to the storehouse where you're spiritually fed. If you have concerns about your church's financial stewardship, address those separately, but don't withhold the tithe as leverage.

Discussion Questions:

1. Where does God want us to bring our tithe as a married couple?

Discuss practically: Which church will be your spiritual home? If you're both already members of the same church, this is straightforward. If not, you'll need to decide together where you'll attend and serve as a couple. That's where your tithe should go.

---

2. How will we decide if we attend different churches?

This situation should be temporary. Ideally, married couples worship together at one church. If you're currently attending different churches, use your engagement period to visit each other's churches, pray together, and decide on one church for your marriage. Then commit your tithe there.

If you must continue attending different churches for a season (perhaps due to work schedules or other temporary factors), discuss how you'll handle the tithe: Will you split it between two churches? Will you tithe to one church and give offerings to the other? The goal should be eventual unity in one church home.

---

3. What if we want to support multiple ministries?

This is wonderful - but do it through your offerings beyond the tithe, not by fragmenting your tithes. The tithe goes to the local church. Additional giving to missionaries, parachurch ministries, crisis pregnancy centers, Christian schools, or other causes should come from generous offerings above the 10%. This honors the storehouse principle while allowing you to support various kingdom works.

Part D: The Purpose and Promise of Tithing

Teaching: Why God Commands Tithing

Tithing isn't arbitrary. God doesn't need your money—He owns "the cattle on a thousand hills" (Psalm 50:10). So why does He command tithing? What purposes does it serve, and what promises accompany faithful tithing?

God's Challenge and Promise: Read Malachi 3:8-12 together

"Will a man rob God? Yet you have robbed Me! But you say, 'In what way have we robbed You?' In tithes and offerings. You are cursed with a curse, for you have robbed Me, even this whole nation. Bring all the tithes into the storehouse, that there may be food in My house, and try Me now in this,' says the Lord of hosts, 'If I will not open for you the windows of heaven and pour out for you such blessing that there will not be room enough to receive it. And I will rebuke the devourer for your sakes, so that he will not destroy the fruit of your ground, nor shall the vine fail to bear fruit for you in the field,' says the Lord of hosts; 'And all nations will call you blessed, for you will be a delightful land,' says the Lord of hosts."

This is one of the most powerful - and sobering - passages about tithing in Scripture. Let's break it down:

The Accusation: Robbing God (v. 8)

God doesn't mince words: withholding tithes is robbery. Not negligence, not financial hardship, not wise stewardship - robbery. This reveals how seriously God views the tithe. When you keep what belongs to Him, you're stealing from God Himself.

The Consequence: A Curse (v. 9)

There's a curse associated with not tithing. This doesn't mean God actively punishes non-tithers, but it does mean that when you rob God, you remove yourself from the place of blessing and protection. You position yourself outside of His promised provision.

The Command: Bring ALL the Tithes (v. 10a)

"Bring all the tithes into the storehouse" means:

- **ALL**: Not partial tithing, not occasional tithing, but full, consistent tithing
- **Into the storehouse**: To your local church, not scattered among various ministries
- **That there may be food in My house**: So that ministry can function

The Invitation: Test Me (v. 10b)

This is the only place in Scripture where God invites us to test Him. "Try Me now in this...if I will not open for you the windows of heaven." God is so confident in His faithfulness that He says, "Put Me to the test. Tithe faithfully and watch what I'll do."

The Promise: Overwhelming Blessing (v. 10c-12)

God promises three specific results of faithful tithing:

Key Purposes of the Tithe:

1. To Support Ministry - "That there may be food in My house" (v. 10)

The first purpose is practical: tithing funds ministry. Pastors, missionaries, worship leaders, children's workers, and countless others depend on tithes to live while they serve God's people full-time. Your tithe provides:

- Pastoral salaries so ministers can focus on spiritual care rather than working secular jobs
- Building maintenance and facilities for worship and ministry
- Resources for teaching, discipleship, and outreach
- Support for missionaries and church planting
- Benevolence for those in crisis

When you tithe, you're investing in the advancement of God's kingdom through the local church.

2. To Position Ourselves for Blessing - "And try Me now in this" (v. 10)

Tithing is a test of faith and obedience. When you tithe, you're declaring: "God, I trust You more than I trust my paycheck. I believe You'll provide for all my needs even after I give You Your portion first."

This act of faith positions you to receive God's blessing. Not because you're buying blessing (you can't manipulate God), but because obedience always positions us to receive what God wants to give. When you hold back the tithe, you're essentially saying, "I don't trust You, God. I need to keep this money to take care of myself." That posture closes you off from blessing.

3. To Experience God's Protection - "I will rebuke the devourer for your sakes" (v. 11)

God promises to "rebuke the devourer"—to protect your finances from unexpected losses, broken appliances, medical emergencies, and the countless ways money seems to disappear. Many faithful tithers testify that their 90% goes farther than 100% used to go before they tithed.

The "devourer" isn't just financial—it can be anything that consumes your resources: chronic car problems, health issues, constantly replacing broken items, bad financial decisions. God promises protection from these devourers when you honor Him with the tithe.

4. To Become a Testimony - "All nations will call you blessed" (v. 12)

Your financial blessing becomes a testimony to God's faithfulness. When unbelievers see that you tithe and yet prosper, when they notice you have peace about finances despite giving away 10%, it points them to God. Your faithfulness in tithing makes you "a delightful land"—attractive and compelling to those watching.

Additional Promises: Read Proverbs 3:9-10

"Honor the Lord with your possessions, and with the firstfruits of all your increase; so your barns will be filled with plenty, and your vats will overflow with new wine."

This passage adds another dimension:

"Honor the Lord with your possessions": Tithing is fundamentally about honor. It's recognizing that everything you have comes from God and honoring Him by returning His portion.

"With the firstfruits of all your increase": Again, the emphasis on first fruits—priority giving, not leftovers.

"So your barns will be filled with plenty, and your vats will overflow": The result is abundance - not just barely enough, but overflowing provision. This doesn't promise luxury or wealth, but it does promise God's generous provision for those who honor Him financially.

Part E: Offerings

Teaching: Understanding the Difference

Many Christians confuse tithes and offerings, treating all "giving" as the same. But Scripture distinguishes between them, and understanding this distinction is important for faithful stewardship.

Understanding the Difference:

Tithes: The first 10% - belongs to God

The tithe is:

- **Obligatory**: It's not optional; it belongs to God
- **Specific**: Exactly 10% of your income
- **Designated**: Goes to your local church (the storehouse)

- **First fruits**: Given from the first portion, not leftovers
- **Foundational**: The baseline of faithful stewardship

When you tithe, you're not being generous - you're being obedient. You're returning to God what already belongs to Him. It's like returning a library book; the book was never yours to keep.

Offerings: Gifts beyond the tithe - freewill expressions of love

Offerings are:

- **Voluntary**: Given from the heart, not obligatory
- **Variable**: No set percentage; you determine the amount
- **Flexible**: Can go to various ministries and causes
- **Generous**: Given from what remains after tithing
- **Worshipful**: True expressions of love and gratitude

Offerings might include:

- Additional giving to your local church beyond the tithe
- Support for missionaries
- Donations to Christian ministries or charities
- Special needs in your community
- Building funds or special projects at your church
- Helping individuals in crisis

Building Fund/Special Projects: Usually supported through offerings

When your church has a building campaign, missions project, or special need, this is typically funded through offerings beyond the tithe. The tithe covers ongoing ministry operations; offerings enable expansion, special projects, and additional ministry.

The Biblical Pattern:

Throughout Scripture, tithes and offerings are mentioned together but distinctly:

- Malachi 3:8: "In tithes and offerings"
- Deuteronomy 12:6: "You shall bring your burnt offerings, your sacrifices, your tithes, the heave offerings of your hand, your vowed offerings, your freewill offerings"

- 2 Chronicles 31:12: "Then they faithfully brought in the offerings, the tithes, and the dedicated things"

The pattern is clear: tithes are the foundation; offerings are the expression of generous worship beyond the foundation.

Couple Planning Session:

1. How much do we currently give in tithes and offerings?

Each person should share honestly:

- Do you currently tithe? If so, on gross or net income?
- How consistent is your tithing - every paycheck, occasionally, rarely?
- Do you give offerings beyond the tithe? How much and to what causes?
- What's your total giving as a percentage of income?

If neither of you currently tithes, this is your opportunity to start fresh as a married couple. If one tithes and the other doesn't, discuss how to move toward unity.

2. What will our tithing commitment be as a married couple?

Make a specific commitment together:

- We will tithe 10% of our combined gross income
- We will tithe on every paycheck/source of income
- We will give our tithe to [name of church]
- We will calculate and give our tithe before paying any other expenses
- We will review our giving regularly to ensure we're staying faithful

Write this commitment down and sign it together. This becomes your covenant of faithful stewardship.

3. How will we handle our giving budget and decisions?

Discuss logistics:

- Will you write one check together or give separately?
- Will you give electronically, by check, or cash?
- How will you track your giving for tax purposes?
- Who will be responsible for ensuring the tithe is given?
- How will you make decisions about offerings - together or independently?
- What system will you use to ensure consistency?

4. What other ministries or causes do we want to support with offerings?

Brainstorm together:

- What missionaries or ministries are you passionate about?
- What local needs burden your heart?
- What percentage or amount do you want to give in offerings beyond the tithe?
- How will you decide together about one-time giving opportunities?

Create a rough budget for giving: 10% tithe to your church, plus X% for offerings to various causes.

Part F: Practical Tithing in Marriage

Teaching: Making It Work Practically

Understanding the theology of tithing is crucial, but faithful stewardship requires practical implementation. How do you actually tithe when bills are due, money is tight, and life gets complicated?

Creating Your Giving Plan:

1. Calculate 10% of your combined gross income

Sit down together with pay stubs or income records and calculate:

- What is each person's gross monthly income?
- What is your combined gross monthly income?
- What is 10% of that amount?

Example:

- Person A gross income: $3,500/month
- Person B gross income: $2,800/month
- Combined gross income: $6,300/month
- Monthly tithe: $630

This is your baseline giving commitment. Everything else in your budget must work around this priority, not the other way around.

2. Plan for tithing on irregular income (bonuses, gifts, tax refunds)

Don't forget to tithe on irregular income:

- **Bonuses**: 10% of your annual bonus
- **Tax refunds**: 10% of your refund (some argue this money was already taxed and tithed on; others argue it's additional income in your hand)
- **Gifts of money**: 10% of cash gifts received (wedding gifts, inheritance, etc.)
- **Raises**: Adjust your tithe when your income increases
- **Business income or self-employment**: 10% of your net profit after business expenses

Create a plan for how you'll handle these irregular income events, so you don't forget to honor God when windfalls come.

3. Discuss your heart attitude toward giving

This is crucial. God cares about the heart behind the gift, not just the amount. Second Corinthians 9:7 says, "So let each one give as he purposes in his heart, not grudgingly or of necessity; for God loves a cheerful giver."

Ask each other:

- Do I give joyfully or resentfully?
- Do I trust God's provision or worry about having enough?
- Do I view tithing as obligation or opportunity?
- Do I give to be blessed or to bless God?
- Am I generous-hearted or stingy-spirited?

If your heart isn't right, pray about it. Ask God to transform your attitude toward giving. The goal isn't just to tithe, it's to become a generous person who delights in honoring God with their resources.

Overcoming Common Challenges:

Challenge 1: "We can't afford to tithe" - How does God's math work?

This is the most common objection, and it often feels legitimate. When bills exceed income, giving away 10% seems financially irresponsible, even impossible.

But consider God's math vs. human math:

Human Math:

- Income: $3,000
- Expenses: $3,200
- Conclusion: We're already $200 short, we can't afford to give away $300!

God's Math:

- Income: $3,000
- Tithe: $300 (given first)
- Remaining: $2,700
- God's promise: He'll make the $2,700 cover what $3,000 couldn't

Countless Christians testify to this reality: once they started tithing in faith, their finances worked better than before. Not always through increased income (though that happens too), but through:

- Unexpected provision at just the right time
- Bills that don't arrive as expected
- Things lasting longer than they should
- Wisdom to reduce expenses they didn't realize were wasteful
- Protection from the "devourer"- fewer financial emergencies

The real question isn't "Can I afford to tithe?" but "Can I afford not to tithe?" When you withhold the tithe, you lose God's blessing and protection. When you honor Him first, He promises to provide.

If you genuinely cannot pay basic necessities after tithing, the issue probably isn't the tithe - it's your spending, your income level, or your debt load. Address those underlying issues rather than excusing yourself from tithing. Perhaps you need:

- To reduce expenses dramatically
- To increase income through additional work
- To tackle debt aggressively
- To seek financial counseling

But don't use financial pressure as a permanent excuse to rob God.

Challenge 2: "I'll tithe when I have more money" - Why first fruits matter

This reasoning seems prudent: "Once I get out of debt, once I get a raise, once I have savings built up - Then I'll start tithing."

But this is backwards. Tithing isn't the reward for financial success; it's the pathway to financial blessing. When you wait until you "have enough," you're trusting in your own provision rather than God's. You're essentially saying, "I need to get financially secure on my own, and then I'll trust God."

Proverbs 3:9 says "firstfruits," not "extra fruits" or "comfortable fruits." God wants priority, not leftovers. When you give Him the first portion even when money is tight, you demonstrate radical trust.

Many people who waited to tithe discover that "enough" never comes. There's always another expense, another goal, another reason to delay. The evil one will always set challenges. Meanwhile, these same people can miss years of God's blessings and the spiritual growth that comes from trusting Him financially.

The time to start tithing is now, regardless of your financial situation. Start where you are, trust God with the results, and watch what He does.

Challenge 3: "My spouse doesn't believe in tithing" - How to handle disagreement

This is particularly challenging. If you're both Christians but one believes in tithing and the other doesn't, you have a theological disagreement that affects practical finances.

If you're not yet married:

Address this during engagement before you combine finances. Study Scripture together, talk to your pastor, and work toward unity. If you can't reach agreement, consider whether you should proceed with marriage - not because tithing is more important than marriage, but because this disagreement reveals deeper issues about biblical authority, trust in God, and financial values.

Principles for navigating disagreement:

1. **Don't tithe secretly or manipulate**: If your spouse opposes tithing, don't hide money or manipulate the budget to tithe without their knowledge. This violates trust and models poor partnership.
2. **Study together with humility**: Approach Scripture together, asking God to reveal His truth to both of you. Be willing to have your view challenged.
3. **Seek counsel together**: Talk to your pastor, a mature Christian couple, or a biblical financial counselor together.
4. **Consider a compromise as a starting point**: If your spouse isn't ready for 10%, perhaps they'd be willing to start with 5% and increase over time as God proves faithful. Not ideal, but better than nothing.
5. **Pray consistently**: Pray for your spouse's heart and your own. Ask God to create unity and to prove His faithfulness.
6. **Model generosity**: If you can't tithe jointly, be generous in other ways that your spouse can see. Your joyful generosity may soften their heart over time.

If one spouse is a believer and the other is not, this becomes even more complex due to the biblical principle of being "unevenly yoked." The believing spouse should pray for wisdom, model faithful stewardship, and trust God to work in the unbelieving spouse's heart. Don't sacrifice marital unity over tithing but also don't stop pursuing God's best.

Action Steps:

1. Calculate what your tithe should be based on current income

Right now, before moving forward, do the math:

- Person A's gross monthly income: $________
- Person B's gross monthly income: $________
- Combined gross monthly income: $________
- Monthly tithe (10%): $________
- Annual tithe: $________

Write these numbers down. See them in black and white. This is your tithe commitment as a couple.

---

2. Decide together where you will tithe as a married couple

Make a specific decision:

We commit to giving our tithe to: _________________________________ (name of church)

If you're currently at different churches, set a deadline for deciding which church will be your joint church home: _________________ (date)

3. Set up a system for consistent, faithful giving

Choose your method and implement it:

- [ ] Set up automatic online giving from our bank account
- [ ] Put tithing on our calendar as the first "bill" we pay each month
- [ ] Designate one person to ensure the tithe is given (who: _________)
- [ ] Track our giving for tax purposes using: _________________
- [ ] Review our giving quarterly to ensure we're staying faithful

The system you create should make tithing automatic and consistent, removing the temptation to skip it when money is tight.

---

4. Pray together about your commitment to biblical stewardship

Before concluding this chapter, pray together. Use this prayer as a guide, or pray in your own words:

Prayer Focus:

"Father, we acknowledge that everything we have comes from You. You are our source, our provider, and our ultimate security. Thank You for the privilege of earning income and for the opportunity to honor You with our finances.

We commit today to be faithful tithers, giving You the first 10% of all our income. We recognize that the tithe belongs to You, and we choose to return it faithfully to Your house. We trust Your promise to open the windows of heaven and pour out blessing, to rebuke the devourer, and to make us a testimony of Your faithfulness.

Help us to give joyfully, not grudgingly. Increase our faith to trust You with our finances even when it requires sacrifice. Protect us from the love of money and the temptation to trust in wealth rather than in You. Make us generous people who delight in giving.

As we prepare for marriage, unite our hearts in faithful stewardship. Help us to honor You first in our finances and to experience Your abundant provision. May our tithing be an act of worship that demonstrates our trust in Your goodness. Use our obedience to advance Your kingdom and bless others.

We ask this in Jesus' name, the One who gave everything for us. Amen."

Closing Reflection: First Things First

Tithing is fundamentally about priorities. When you give God the first tenth of your income before paying any other expense, you're making a declaration: "God, You are first in my life, not just in theory but in practice. I trust You more than I trust my ability to manage money. I believe Your promises and I'm positioning myself to receive Your blessing."

This act of faith pleases God. Hebrews 11:6 says, "Without faith it is impossible to please Him, for he who comes to God must believe that He is, and that He is a rewarder of those who diligently seek Him." Tithing is an expression of faith—believing that God exists, that He rewards faithfulness, and that His ways work even when they contradict human wisdom.

As you prepare for marriage, establish tithing as a non-negotiable foundation of your financial life together. When you honor God first with your finances, you invite His blessing, protection, and provision into your marriage. When you withhold the tithe, you rob yourself of the very blessing you need to prosper.

The couple who tithes faithfully, regardless of their income level, positions themselves for God's blessing. They demonstrate trust that transcends circumstances. They model for future children what it means to honor God practically. They invest in kingdom work that has eternal significance. And they experience the joy of participating in what God is doing through their local church.

Make the decision today: You will be faithful tithers. Your marriage will be built on the foundation of honoring God first with your finances. And as you do, watch what God does. He's promised to open the windows of heaven and pour out blessing—and God keeps His promises.

CHAPTER 8: GOD'S DESIGN FOR SEXUALITY IN MARRIAGE

Few topics generate more confusion, anxiety, and misconception than sexuality and more so as sexuality relates to the Christian and Christian marriages. Our culture bombards us with distorted messages about sex: that it's merely physical, that personal satisfaction is the ultimate goal, that any consensual act is acceptable, and that sexual "compatibility" should be tested before marriage. Even within the church, sexuality is often addressed with either awkward silence or legalistic warnings that leave couples unprepared for this vital dimension of marriage.

But God is not silent about sexuality. He created it. He designed it for specific purposes within specific boundaries. And when couples understand and embrace His design, they discover that marital intimacy is far more profound, satisfying, and meaningful than the world's cheap counterfeits.

God designed sexuality within marriage to be a beautiful and sacred expression of unity between husband and wife. His design is all-embracing. God's design for sexuality in marriage touches every part of who we are: physical, emotional, relational, and spiritual. Sex is not merely a physical act; it's an encompassing union that engages the totality of two people becoming one flesh.

In this chapter, we'll explore how four unique elements of intimacy (Physical, Emotional, Relational, Spiritual) work together under the umbrella of the four biblical essentials (Mutuality, Oneness, Honor/Respect, No Shame) that support mutual fulfillment. Couples will discover that God's design for sexuality is not restrictive but protective, not limiting but liberating. When couples build their intimate life on His foundation, they experience the freedom, joy, and deep connection that He intended from the beginning.

Main Scripture:

"For this reason, a man shall leave his father and his mother and be joined to his wife; and they shall become one flesh." Genesis 2:24 (NASB)

This verse, spoken before sin entered the world, reveals God's original design: a man and woman leaving their families of origin, being permanently joined in covenant, and becoming one flesh. The "one flesh" union encompasses far more than physical intercourse. The "one flesh" describes the thorough merging of two lives, two identities, and two persons into a new unified whole.

Part A: The Four Elements of Marital Intimacy

Teaching: Understanding Complete Intimacy

Many couples enter marriage thinking sexuality is primarily physical. This limited understanding in many cases leads to disappointment and disconnection. God's design engages the totality of who we are and does so through Four Elements.

The Four Elements:

1. **Physical** – The bodily expression of love and unity

2. **Emotional** – The sharing of feelings, affection, and trust

3. **Relational** – The bond of companionship and partnership

4. **Spiritual** – The sacred reflection of God's covenant love

These elements are interwoven like threads that strengthen onc another. When one is weak, intimacy suffers. When all four are nurtured, sexual intimacy becomes what God intended: a profound, multidimensional expression of the marriage covenant of love.

Part B: God's Four Elements of Sexuality in Marriage

Element 1: Physical -The Bodily Expression of Love and Unity

The physical dimension is God's good gift to marriage. Your body is "fearfully and wonderfully made" (Psalm 139:14) and designed for mutual pleasure as well as procreation within the covenant.

Scripture: "Do you not know that your body is a temple of the Holy Spirit... therefore glorify God in your body." 1 Corinthians 6:19-20

Key Aspects:

- Physical union expresses love in ways words cannot

- In marriage, spouses give their bodies to one another for mutual benefit and delight (1 Corinthians 7:4)

- Physical compatibility grows through patient communication

- God celebrates physical pleasure in marriage (Proverbs 5:18-19, Song of Solomon)

The physical element reminds us that our bodies matter to God and that sexual expression is a way of honoring Him when it reflects love, respect, and mutual care.

Element 2: Emotional—The Sharing of Feelings, Affection, and Trust

Sexual intimacy requires emotional vulnerability and safety. You cannot fully give yourself physically to someone you don't trust emotionally.

Scripture: "Be devoted to one another in love. Honor one another above yourselves." Romans 12:10

Key Aspects:

- Emotional safety is foundational in marriage. Fear or criticism creates barriers

- Vulnerability deepens connections as you share fears, desires, and dreams with your spouse

- Affection extends beyond the bedroom through daily expressions of that same caring

- Past wounds affect present intimacy and may require professional help

The Emotional Element teaches us that sexual intimacy cannot be separated from the emotional health of the marriage.

Element 3: Relational - The Bond of Companionship and Partnership

What happens in the marriage bed is deeply connected to how spouses relate in everyday life.

Scripture: "Then the LORD God said, 'It is not good for the man to be alone; I will make him a helper suitable for him.'" - Genesis 2:18

Key Aspects:

- Intimacy grows from friendship - couples who enjoy each other's company have stronger foundations

- Communication about desires and expectations prevents misunderstanding

- Unresolved conflict creates distance that affects physical intimacy

- Partnership extends to the bedroom as spouses work together to meet each other's needs

The Relational Element reminds each of us that if we wish a better intimate relationship, we need to become better friends.

Element 4: Spiritual - The Sacred Reflection of God's Covenant Love

Sexual intimacy reflects the covenant relationship between Christ and the Church and invites God's presence into the most intimate moments of marriage.

Scriptures: "This mystery is profound, and I am saying that it refers to Christ and the church." Ephesians 5:32

"Unless the LORD builds the house, those who build it labor in vain." Psalm 127:1

Key Aspects:

- Marriage mirrors divine love - the one-flesh union is a living picture of the gospel

- Intimacy can be an act of worship when approached with reverence and gratitude

- Shared faith deepens intimacy as couples pray and seek God together

- God's presence sanctifies the marriage bed (Hebrews 13:4)

The spiritual element elevates sexual intimacy beyond physical pleasure into a sign of the sacred covenant expression.

How the Four Elements Work Together

Like a four-strand cord, these elements strengthen one another:

- Physical intimacy without emotional connection becomes hollow

- Emotional vulnerability without relational friendship lacks foundation

- Relational partnership without spiritual grounding misses its ultimate purpose

- Spiritual unity without physical expression remains incomplete

When all four are present and nurtured, sexual intimacy brings glory to God and deep fulfillment to both spouses.

Part C: Four Biblical Essentials

These Four Biblical Essentials provide the framework within which the Four Elements flourish.

Essential 1: Mutuality

While either spouse may initiate, both must agree to any sexual behavior.

Scripture: "The husband must fulfill his duty to his wife, and likewise also the wife to her husband... Do not deprive one another except by agreement for a time..." 1 Corinthians 7:3-5

- Neither spouse should feel forced, controlled, or used
- Each seeks to lovingly meet the other's needs
- Preferences are discussed and respected

Essential 2: Oneness

Sexual intimacy strengthens the marital bond, transforming "me" into "we."

Scripture: "For this reason a man shall leave his father and his mother and shall be joined to his wife; and they shall become one flesh." Genesis 2:24

- Sexual intimacy deepens unity and expresses the mystery of one flesh
- Each union reinforces exclusivity and commitment
- Nothing should intrude on this sacred space (no pornography, fantasies about others, etc.)

Essential 3: Honor/Respect

Each spouse should feel valued and cherished, placing the other's well-being first.

Scriptures: "Let your fountain be blessed and rejoice in the wife of your youth... be intoxicated always in her love." Proverbs 5:18-19

"Marriage is honorable among all, and the bed undefiled..." Hebrews 13:4

- Marriage intimacy is built on love, respect, and faithfulness

- Your spouse should feel treasured before, during, and after intimacy

- Never criticize, compare, or pressure your spouse

Essential 4: No Shame

God's design allows couples to enjoy one another freely without shame.

Scriptures: "And the man and his wife were both naked and were not ashamed." Genesis 2:25

"You are altogether beautiful, my love; there is no flaw in you." Song of Solomon 4:7

- True intimacy brings freedom, acceptance, and delight

- Both spouses can be fully vulnerable without fear of rejection

- Past shame (from abuse, sin, or cultural messages) needs healing

---

Part D: Sexual Personalities in Marriage

Each spouse brings a unique sexual personality with them into the marriage. This unique personality has been shaped by past experiences, beliefs, and temperament. These all work to affect how each spouse expresses love and intimacy. However, not all expressions align with God's design for marriage. Those that align with Gods design are called "In Bound Expressions," and those that do not align with God's design are called "Out of Bounds Expressions."

In Bounds Expressions vs. Out of Bounds Expressions

In Bounds Expressions (Biblical / Constructive)	Out of Bounds Expressions (Sinful / Destructive)
Pleasure	Adultery
Procreation	Pornography
Companionship	Homosexual Acts
Mutual Sharing	Bestiality
Freedom	Incest
Intimacy	Prostitution
	Lust / Self-Gratification
	Abuse / Coercion
	Fornication

Key Insight: In Bounds Expressions align with God's design for marriage - leading to oneness and blessings. Out of Bounds Expressions pursue self-gratification, damage intimacy and separate the couple from God's blessings. Not all Expressions are "black" and "white" however. Some come under the heading of Gray Areas. Here is some guidance on seeking resolution to any Gray Areas.

For Gray Areas, Ask:

1. Is it mutual? Do both genuinely desire it?

2. Is it honoring? Do both feel valued?

3. Is it exclusive? Only the two of you?

4. Is it beneficial? Does it strengthen your bond?

5. Is it without shame? Can you do it with clear conscience?

Reflection Questions:

1. Which of the Four Essentials (Mutuality, Oneness, Honor/Respect, No Shame) do you feel strongest in? Which of them needs growth?

2. How have past experiences shaped your view of sexuality?

3. What does it mean to you that your marriage reflects the image of God?

4. How can you protect your marriage bed and keep intimacy "in bounds"?

Action Steps:

1. Study Scripture Together Here are some great Scriptures. Read them together: Genesis 2:18-25, 1 Corinthians 7:3-5, Proverbs 5:15-19, Song of Solomon selections, and Hebrews 13:4. Discuss what these reveal about God's design.

2. Discuss Your Backgrounds Share how you were taught about sexuality growing up and how it has shaped your views. (Keep the discussion general in nature and leave out specifics)

3. Identify Areas Needing Healing If either of you carries wounds related to sexuality, create a plan for healing through counseling and prayer. Your advisor can work with you with resources and refer you for biblical counseling.

4. Establish Protective Boundaries Agree now on immoveable boundaries: no pornography, complete mutual accountability for all electronic devices including mutual sharing of passwords, agreement about entertainment choices, how each of you will handle attraction towards others.

5. Pray Together This is so important! Invite the Holy Spirit in to align your hearts with God's Word regarding intimacy. Pray for healing, protection, and mutual fulfillment.

Closing Reflection

When intimacy reflects God's heart, it fulfills both the Four Elements (Physical, Emotional, Relational, Spiritual) and the Four Essentials (Mutuality, Oneness, Honor/Respect, No Shame). These work in harmony to bring unity, joy, and spiritual wholeness into the marriage.

When a marriage drifts outside these bounds, intimacy becomes self-focused - driven by "How can this marriage fulfill my needs, my wants, my desires?" In this state, the marriage cannot reflect God's purpose of two becoming one flesh.

But when couples embrace God's design, something beautiful happens. Sexual intimacy becomes:

- A physical expression of covenant love

- An emotional experience of deep knowing and being known

- A relational bond that strengthens friendship and partnership

- A spiritual act of worship that glorifies God

This is how God intended the Marriage Covenant from the beginning - two people, fully committed, fully vulnerable, fully united in body, soul, and spirit. It's a gift beyond what the world can offer because it's rooted in something the world doesn't have: covenant faithfulness that reflects Christ's love for the Church.

A Word of Caution:

If you're currently struggling with sexual sin - pornography use, sexual activity with your fiancé, emotional affairs, or other issues - address these areas now, before marriage. Don't assume marriage will fix these problems. It won't. In fact, unaddressed sexual sin often gets worse after marriage because you've established patterns that carry forward.

Confess to your fiancé (<u>with appropriate boundaries about details</u>), seek accountability, and get help. Your future marriage is worth the difficult conversations and hard work required now to enter it with integrity.

Final Reflection Questions:

Before concluding this chapter, take time to reflect individually and then discuss together:

1. **What is your biggest takeaway from this chapter?** What truth do you most need to remember as you prepare for the sexual dimension of marriage?

2. **What concerns or fears do you have about sexual intimacy in marriage?** How can you address these proactively?

3. **How will you cultivate all Four Elements (Physical, Emotional, Relational, Spiritual) in your intimate life?**

4. **How will you maintain the Four Essentials (Mutuality, Oneness, Honor/Respect, No Shame) throughout your marriage?**

5. **What boundaries and protections will you put in place to keep your marriage bed pure and honoring to God?**

Closing Prayer:

"Father, thank You for the gift of marriage and the beauty of intimacy as You designed it. Teach us to honor one another, to love selflessly, and to walk in purity. Heal any wounds we carry. Protect our marriage from anything that would compromise its purity.

Protect our future marriage from the attacks of the enemy. Guard us from pornography, from wandering eyes, from anything that would compromise the exclusivity and purity of our union. Build a hedge around our marriage bed.

May our intimate life reflect Your heart, Your faithfulness, Your self-giving love, Your covenant commitment. May our union bring glory to Your name and deep fulfillment to both of us. We commit this area of our marriage to You, trusting that as we follow Your design, we'll experience all the blessings You intend.

May our union reflect Your heart and bring You glory. In Jesus' name, Amen."

Additional Resources:

Recommended Reading:

- **Sheet Music** by Dr. Kevin Leman

- **Intended for Pleasure** by Ed Wheat, M.D.

- **The Gift of Sex** by Clifford and Joyce Penner

For Those with Past Wounds:

- **Rid of My Disgrace** by Justin and Lindsey Holcomb

- **Surfing for God** by Michael John Cusick (for men and pornography)

Note to Couples: This chapter addresses sensitive and deeply personal topics. If working through this material has raised significant concerns - about your own past, your fiancé's past, or your readiness to navigate this dimension of marriage - please speak with your facilitator. Some couples benefit from additional counseling before marriage to address sexual wounds, establish healthy patterns, or work through significant differences in expectations.

There is no shame in seeking help. In fact, pursuing healing and wholeness before marriage is one of the wisest investments you can make in your future together.

APPENDICES

Recommended Resources for Marriage Preparation

APPENDIX A: RECOMMENDED READING FOR COUPLES

Essential Reading (Highly Recommended)

The Meaning of Marriage by Timothy Keller A profound exploration of the biblical vision for marriage that addresses cultural misconceptions while presenting marriage as a reflection of the gospel. Excellent for engaged couples seeking theological depth.

Sacred Marriage by Gary Thomas Challenges the idea that marriage's primary purpose is happiness, asking instead: "What if God designed marriage to make us holy more than to make us happy?" Prepares couples for the sanctifying nature of marriage.

Love & Respect by Dr. Emerson Eggerichs Based on Ephesians 5:33, this book explores how husbands need respect and wives need love, and how understanding this dynamic transforms marriage. Practical and biblically grounded.

The Five Love Languages by Gary Chapman Helps couples understand how they give and receive love differently. Essential for learning to love your spouse in ways they actually feel loved.

Boundaries in Marriage by Dr. Henry Cloud & Dr. John Townsend Teaches how to establish healthy boundaries that protect the marriage while maintaining individual identity and responsibility. Crucial for couples from dysfunctional backgrounds.

Additional Recommended Reading

Sheet Music by Dr. Kevin Leman A Christian perspective on sexual intimacy in marriage. Frank, biblical, and helpful for couples preparing for the physical dimension of marriage.

His Needs, Her Needs by Willard F. Harley Jr. Identifies the top needs of husbands and wives and how meeting those needs prevents affairs and strengthens marriage.

The Mingling of Souls by Matt Chandler A shorter, accessible book on God's design for love, marriage, sex, and redemption. Great for couples who struggle with longer books.

Preparing for Marriage by Dennis Rainey A comprehensive workbook covering communication, finances, sexuality, and roles. Can be used alongside this workbook for additional exercises.

For Women: The Excellent Wife by Martha Peace Biblical perspective on a wife's role with practical application. Reformed/complementarian perspective.

For Men: The Exemplary Husband by Stuart Scott Companion to *The Excellent Wife*, focusing on the husband's biblical responsibilities. Reformed/complementarian perspective.

Created to Be His Help Meet by Debi Pearl Focuses on the wife's role as helper. Note: This book has a very traditional perspective that some find extreme. Use discernment.

APPENDIX B: RECOMMENDED READING FOR FACILITATORS

Marriage Counseling Resources

Preparing Couples for Love and Marriage by Jeff & Debbie McElroy A comprehensive guide for pastors and counselors conducting pre-marriage counseling, with biblical foundations and practical tools.

Premarital Counseling by H. Norman Wright Classic resource covering assessment, major topics, and counseling techniques. Includes reproducible forms and questionnaires.

The Peacemaker by Ken Sande Essential for teaching conflict resolution biblically. Chapter 2 ("The Slippery Slope") alone is worth the book's price for understanding how conflicts escalate.

Instruments in the Redeemer's Hands by Paul David Tripp Foundational book on biblical counseling that helps advisors understand how to guide people toward change through Scripture.

The Pastor's Guide to Performing Premarital Counseling by Harry Wendt Short, practical guide specifically for pastors, addressing legal requirements, ceremony planning, and counseling structure.

Marriage Theology

This Momentary Marriage by John Piper Short, powerful meditation on marriage's purpose in light of eternity. Helps advisors maintain proper perspective on what marriage is ultimately about.

Marriage and the Mystery of the Gospel by Ray Ortlund Explores how marriage reflects Christ and the church, providing deep theological grounding for advisors.

God, Marriage, and Family by Andreas J. Köstenberger Comprehensive biblical theology of marriage and family, addressing roles, singleness, divorce/remarriage, parenting, and contemporary issues.

Financial Counseling

The Total Money Makeover by Dave Ramsey Practical framework for getting out of debt and building financial stability. Helpful for couples with significant financial challenges.

Financial Peace University by Dave Ramsey Complete course covering budgeting, debt elimination, saving, and giving. Can supplement chapters 6-7 of this workbook.

Your Money Counts by Howard Dayton Biblical principles of financial stewardship with practical application. More explicitly Christian than Ramsey's work.

APPENDIX C: ASSESSMENT TOOLS & INVENTORIES

Personality Assessments

DISC Assessment

- Measures Dominance, Influence, Steadiness, Conscientiousness
- Quick, easy to understand, workplace-applicable
- Multiple free versions available online
- Recommended for Chapter 5

Myers-Briggs Type Indicator (MBTI)

- 16 personality types based on four dichotomies
- Deeper than DISC, more complex
- Official version requires payment; free alternatives (16Personalities.com)
- Good for understanding communication and decision-making styles

Enneagram

- Nine personality types focused on core motivations
- Increasingly popular in Christian circles
- Helps identify growth areas and blind spots
- Free tests available; books provide depth

StrengthsFinder (CliftonStrengths)

- Identifies top 5 strengths from 34 themes
- Positive focus on what each person does well
- Requires purchase of book or assessment
- Helpful for identifying complementary abilities

Premarital Inventories

PREPARE/ENRICH

- Comprehensive premarital assessment (165 questions)
- Covers 14 relationship categories
- Requires facilitator certification
- Gold standard for premarital assessment
- Website: prepare-enrich.com

FOCCUS (Facilitating Open Couple Communication, Understanding & Study)

- Catholic-developed but used across denominations
- 156 questions covering major marriage topics
- Identifies agreement/disagreement areas
- Requires facilitator training
- Website: foccusinc.com

SYMBIS (Saving Your Marriage Before It Starts)

- Created by Drs. Les & Leslie Parrott
- Online assessment with personalized report
- Includes 15 comprehensive exercises
- Website: symbis.com

Relationship Evaluation (RELATE)

- Research-based assessment from BYU
- Free version available
- Covers personality, backgrounds, relationship dynamics
- Website: relate-institute.org

Spiritual Gifts Assessments

Spiritual Gifts Test - NewBeginnings *(mentioned in workbook)* Contact your church leadership or search online for "spiritual gifts assessment" to find versions aligned with your theology.

Team Ministry Spiritual Gifts Inventory Free, comprehensive assessment identifying spiritual gifts with biblical references.

LifeWay Spiritual Gifts Survey Free resource from LifeWay Christian Resources, includes gifts discovery process.

APPENDIX D: ONLINE RESOURCES & WEBSITES

Marriage Ministry Organizations

FamilyLife (familylife.com)

- Dennis Rainey's ministry
- Resources for engaged couples, married couples, and families
- Weekend to Remember marriage conferences
- Daily radio broadcasts and podcasts

Focus on the Family (focusonthefamily.com)

- Comprehensive marriage and family resources
- Articles, broadcasts, counseling referrals
- Marriage conferences and events

The Gottman Institute (gottman.com)

- Research-based marriage resources
- Note: Secular organization, but sound research
- Assessment tools and counseling approaches
- Use discernment; filter through biblical lens

Marriage Missions International (marriagemissions.com)

- Large collection of marriage articles
- Topics organized by category
- Free resources for couples and counselors

The Marriage Podcast for Smart People (marriagepodcast.com)

- Dr. Jennifer Finlayson-Fife
- Thoughtful discussions on marriage, sexuality, and relationships
- Note: Some content requires discernment

Financial Resources

Crown Financial Ministries (crown.org)

- Biblical financial teaching and counseling
- Small group studies on stewardship
- Budget tools and resources

Dave Ramsey (daveramsey.com)

- Financial Peace University
- EveryDollar budgeting app
- Debt snowball calculators
- Podcasts and videos

Compass - Finances God's Way (compass1.org)

- Biblical financial teaching
- Small group studies
- MoneyLife Personal Finance Study

Church Resources

The Gospel Coalition (thegospelcoalition.org)

- Articles on marriage, family, theology
- Search "marriage" for relevant content
- Reformed/evangelical perspective

Desiring God (desiringgod.org)

- John Piper's ministry
- Sermons, articles, books on marriage
- "This Momentary Marriage" available free

The Village Church Resources (tvc.org/resources)

- Matt Chandler's church
- Sermons and articles on relationships
- Marriage preparation materials

APPENDIX E: HELPFUL FORMS & WORKSHEETS

Budget Worksheet Template

Monthly Income:

- Salary/Wages (Person 1): $_______
- Salary/Wages (Person 2): $_______
- Other Income: $_______
- **TOTAL GROSS INCOME: $_______**

Giving (10%+ of gross):

- Tithe: $_______
- Offerings: $_______
- **TOTAL GIVING: $_______**

Housing (25-35% of net):

- Mortgage/Rent: $_______
- Property Tax: $_______
- Insurance: $_______
- HOA Fees: $_______
- Utilities (Electric, Gas, Water): $_______
- Internet/Cable: $_______
- Maintenance/Repairs: $_______
- **TOTAL HOUSING: $_______**

Transportation (10-15% of net):

- Car Payment 1: $_______
- Car Payment 2: $_______
- Gas: $_______
- Insurance: $_______
- Maintenance: $_______
- **TOTAL TRANSPORTATION: $_______**

Food (10-15% of net):

- Groceries: $_______
- Restaurants/Eating Out: $_______
- **TOTAL FOOD: $_______**

Insurance:

- Health Insurance: $_______
- Life Insurance: $_______
- Disability Insurance: $_______
- **TOTAL INSURANCE: $_______**

Debt Payments:

- Student Loans: $_______
- Credit Cards: $_______
- Other Debt: $_______
- **TOTAL DEBT: $_______**

Personal/Discretionary:

- Clothing: $_______
- Phone: $_______
- Entertainment: $_______
- Personal Care: $_______
- Gifts: $_______
- Subscriptions: $_______
- **TOTAL PERSONAL: $_______**

Savings:

- Emergency Fund: $_______
- Retirement: $_______
- Other Savings Goals: $_______
- **TOTAL SAVINGS: $_______**

Miscellaneous:

- Medical/Dental: $_______
- Other: $_______
- **TOTAL MISCELLANEOUS: $_______**

TOTAL EXPENSES: $_______

Net Income (Income - Expenses): $_______

Wedding Planning Budget

Use this Hand-Out to help couples maintain realistic expectations about wedding costs while staying out of debt.

Ceremony:

- Venue: $________
- Officiant: $________
- Marriage License: $________
- Music: $________
- Decorations: $________
- **SUBTOTAL: $________**

Reception:

- Venue: $________
- Catering/Food: $________
- Cake: $________
- Decorations: $________
- **SUBTOTAL: $________**

Attire:

- Wedding Dress: $________
- Alterations: $________
- Groom's Attire: $________
- Wedding Party Attire (if paying): $________
- **SUBTOTAL: $________**

Photography/Videography:

- Photographer: $________
- Videographer: $________
- **SUBTOTAL: $________**

Flowers:

- Bridal Bouquet: $________
- Ceremony Flowers: $________
- Reception Centerpieces: $________
- **SUBTOTAL: $________**

Invitations/Paper:

- Save the Dates: $_______
- Invitations: $_______
- Programs: $_______
- Thank You Cards: $_______
- **SUBTOTAL: $_______**

Other:

- Rehearsal Dinner: $_______
- Transportation: $_______
- Favors: $_______
- Gifts for Wedding Party: $_______
- Honeymoon: $_______
- Miscellaneous: $_______
- **SUBTOTAL: $_______**

TOTAL WEDDING BUDGET: $_______

Funding Sources:

- Personal Savings: $_______
- Bride's Family: $_______
- Groom's Family: $_______
- Other: $_______
- **TOTAL FUNDING: $_______**

SHORTFALL/SURPLUS: $_______

Conversation Starters for Deeper Discussions

Use these questions during counseling sessions to go deeper than the workbook alone allows:

Spiritual:

- "Describe a time when God clearly answered your prayer."
- "What's the most significant way your faith has grown in the past year?"
- "How do you hear from God?"
- "What spiritual disciplines do you struggle with most?"

Relational:

- "How did your parents handle conflict? How has that shaped you?"
- "What makes you feel most loved?"
- "When you're upset, do you need space or connection?"
- "What's your biggest fear about marriage?"

Financial:

- "What's the best financial decision you've ever made? The worst?"
- "How much money would make you feel 'secure'?"
- "What are you willing to sacrifice financially? What aren't you willing to sacrifice?"
- "How did your family talk about money growing up?"

Sexual:

- "What are your expectations about sexual frequency in marriage?"
- "Have you discussed your sexual histories with each other?"
- "Are there areas of sexual intimacy you're uncomfortable with?"
- "How will you handle differences in sexual desire?"

Future:

- "Where do you see yourselves in 5 years? 10 years? 20 years?"
- "What does success in marriage look like to you?"
- "What role will your careers play in your marriage priorities?"
- "How will you handle major life transitions (children, aging parents, career changes)?"

APPENDIX F: WHEN TO REFER TO PROFESSIONAL COUNSELING

As an Advisor/Facilitator, you're not equipped to handle every situation. Know when to refer couples to licensed Christian/Biblical Counselors:

Refer for:

- **Mental Health Issues**: Depression, anxiety disorders, PTSD, personality disorders, bipolar disorder, etc.
- **Addiction**: Substance abuse, pornography addiction, gambling, eating disorders
- **Past Trauma**: Sexual abuse, physical abuse, severe neglect, traumatic events
- **Current Abuse**: Any form of abuse in the relationship requires immediate professional intervention
- **Complex Family Systems**: Severe family dysfunction, enmeshment, toxic patterns
- **Unresolved Grief**: Loss of loved ones, miscarriage, previous children lost
- **Sexual Issues**: Sexual dysfunction, past sexual abuse, compulsive sexual behavior

Finding Christian Counselors:

- American Association of Christian Counselors (aacc.net) - counselor directory
- Focus on the Family counseling referral line: 1-855-771-HELP (4357)
- Local Christian counseling centers
- Psychology Today directory (filter for "Christian" or "faith-based")
- Recommendations from other pastors in your area

Making the Referral:

- Be direct but compassionate: "This issue is beyond my training. I want you to get the best help possible."
- Provide specific referrals, not just "find a counselor"
- Offer to continue meeting while they're in counseling if appropriate
- Follow up to ensure they actually made the appointment
- Don't feel like a failure for referring—it's wise stewardship of your limitations

APPENDIX G: LEGAL REQUIREMENTS FOR MARRIAGE

Note: Marriage laws vary by state/country. This is general guidance; couples should verify specific requirements in their jurisdiction.

Typical Requirements:

- Marriage license (obtained from county clerk, usually valid 30-90 days)
- Age requirements (typically 18+, with parental consent for minors where allowed)
- Waiting period (0-3 days depending on state)
- Blood tests (required in very few states now)
- Valid identification
- Officiant authorized to perform marriages
- Witnesses (typically 1-2 required)

As an Officiant, You Need:

- Proper credentials recognized by your state
- Completed marriage license signed by couple and witnesses
- Submission of marriage license to county clerk within required timeframe

Premarital Counseling Requirements: Some states offer marriage license fee discounts or waiting period waivers for couples who complete premarital counseling. Check your state's requirements.

Additional Considerations:

- Name changes (Social Security, driver's license, bank accounts, etc.)
- Insurance beneficiaries
- Wills and estate planning
- Tax implications

APPENDIX H: SAMPLE WEDDING CEREMONY OUTLINE

Processional

- Seating of mothers
- Wedding party entrance
- Bride's entrance

Welcome & Opening Prayer

- Welcome guests
- Acknowledge God's presence and blessing
- Opening prayer

Statement on Marriage

- Brief teaching on biblical marriage
- Marriage as covenant, not contract
- Reflection of Christ and the church

Charge to the Couple

- Reminder of marriage's sacred nature
- Call to faithfulness and perseverance
- Exhortation to build on Christ

Declaration of Intent

- "Who gives this woman to be married?"
- "Do you, [Name], take [Name] to be your lawfully wedded [wife/husband]?"

Scripture Reading

- Suggested passages: Genesis 2:18-24, 1 Corinthians 13, Ephesians 5:22-33, Colossians 3:12-17

Message/Homily

- Brief (5-10 minutes) teaching on marriage
- Gospel-centered
- Practical and encouraging

Exchange of Vows

- Traditional or personalized
- Include covenant language

Exchange of Rings

- Symbol of unending love and commitment

Communion

Unity Elements (Optional)

- Unity candle
- Sand ceremony
- Communion

Pronouncement

- "By the authority vested in me..."
- "I now pronounce you husband and wife"

Prayer of Blessing

- Pray for the couple's marriage
- Invite God's blessing and presence

Presentation

- "I present to you Mr. and Mrs..."

First Kiss

Recessional

APPENDIX I: POST-MARRIAGE FOLLOW-UP

Your role doesn't end at the wedding. Consider these follow-up practices:

1-Month Check-In

- Send encouraging card or email
- Ask how first month has been
- Remind them you're available if needed

3-Month Meeting (Optional but Recommended)

- Schedule brief meeting to discuss adjustment
- Address any issues emerging
- Answer questions they didn't know to ask before marriage

6-Month Check-In

- Phone call or email
- "How's married life?"
- Offer resources if they're struggling

First Anniversary

- Send card acknowledging their first year
- Encourage them to keep investing in their marriage
- Invite them to mentor engaged couples eventually

Ongoing Resources:

- Invite them to church marriage enrichment events
- Recommend marriage conferences (Weekend to Remember, etc.)
- Suggest small groups for married couples
- Be available for crisis counseling if needed

These resources are tools to enhance your marriage preparation ministry. You don't need every resource listed, choose what fits your context, theology, and the specific needs of couples you serve. You may copy and distribute any and all of these Resources. It is my prayer that they will be useful in blessings and enriching both you and your couples.

The most important resources you bring are your own faithfulness to God's Word, your commitment to speak truth in love, and your willingness to invest in your couples' lives. Let these materials serve that calling, not replace it.

Remember: You're not just preparing couples for a wedding day. You're equipping them for a lifetime covenant that will display God's glory for decades to come. This eternal perspective makes all the difference.

May God bless your ministry to engaged couples, and may the marriages you help prepare be strong, Christ-centered, and fruitful for His kingdom.

For Marriage Preparation Facilitators

HOW TO USE THESE FORMS

Form 1 (Initial Intake): Have each person complete separately before first session. Review carefully to identify potential issues before meeting.

Form 2 (Relationship Health): Complete during first 1-2 sessions after getting to know the couple. Use to establish baseline and identify focus areas.

Form 3 (Session Notes): Complete after every session while details are fresh. These notes protect you legally and help track progress.

Form 4 (Final Assessment): Complete after final session to document your recommendation and any ongoing concerns.

Form 5 (Couple Feedback): Have couples complete this to improve your counseling process and identify what's working/not working.

Record Keeping:

- Keep all forms in a secure, confidential file for each couple

- Retain records for at least 7 years (check your state's requirements)

- Never share without written permission (except legally mandated reporting)

- Store electronically with password protection or in locked file cabinet

Legal Protection: These forms document your marriage preparedness process and recommendations. Keep them as a record which can assist in everyone's protection should a couple later question whether they were adequately prepared by you.

FORM 1: INITIAL COUPLE INTAKE FORM

To be completed by each person individually before the first session

Personal Information:

Full Name: ____ Date: ____________

Preferred Name: ____

Date of Birth: _______________ Age: ______

Address: ____

City/State/Zip: ____

Phone: _______________________ Email: _______________________

Occupation: _______________________ Employer: _______________________

Current Relationship Information:

Length of relationship: ___________ Length of engagement: ___________

Wedding date (if set): ___________ Wedding location: _______________

Have you lived together? ☐ Yes ☐ No If yes, for how long? ___________

Are you currently living together? ☐ Yes ☐ No

Spiritual Background:

Current church: ____

How long attending? ___________

Member? ☐ Yes ☐ No Regular attender? ☐ Yes ☐ No

Describe your conversion experience (when/how you became a Christian):

Are you baptized? ☐ Yes ☐ No If yes, when? _____________

Do you currently tithe? ☐ Yes ☐ No If yes, where? _____________________

Current ministry involvement: ____

Previous Relationship History:

Have you been married before? ☐ Yes ☐ No

If yes:

- How many times? ______
- Date(s) of divorce: ___________
- Reason for divorce: ____
- Length of time since divorce: ___________
- Do you have children from previous marriage? ☐ Yes ☐ No

Have you been engaged before? ☐ Yes ☐ No

If yes:

- How many times? ______
- Why did engagement(s) end? _______________________________

Children:

Do you have children? ☐ Yes ☐ No

If yes, please list:

1. Name: _______________ Age: ______ Lives with: ☐ You ☐ Other parent ☐ Shared
2. Name: _______________ Age: ______ Lives with: ☐ You ☐ Other parent ☐ Shared
3. Name: _______________ Age: ______ Lives with: ☐ You ☐ Other parent ☐ Shared

Current child support obligations: $ ___________ per month

Custody arrangement: ____

Family Background:

Parents' marital status: ☐ Married ☐ Divorced ☐ Widowed ☐ Never married ☐ Remarried

If divorced, your age when divorce occurred: ________________

Relationship with father: ☐ Excellent ☐ Good ☐ Fair ☐ Poor ☐ Estranged ☐ Deceased

Relationship with mother: ☐ Excellent ☐ Good ☐ Fair ☐ Poor ☐ Estranged ☐ Deceased

Number of siblings: ______ Your birth order: ______

Any significant family dysfunction? (abuse, addiction, mental illness, etc.)

Health Information:

Current physical health: ☐ Excellent ☐ Good ☐ Fair ☐ Poor

Any chronic health conditions: ____

Current medications: ____

Current mental health: ☐ Excellent ☐ Good ☐ Fair ☐ Poor ☐ Seeking help

Ever been diagnosed with mental health condition? ☐ Yes ☐ No

If yes, specify: ____

Currently in counseling/therapy? ☐ Yes ☐ No

If yes, for what reason? ____

Financial Information:

Current gross annual income: $ ___________

Current debt (total): $ ___________

Types of debt (check all that apply): ☐ Student loans ☐ Credit cards ☐ Car loans
☐ Medical debt ☐ Other: _________________

Credit score (if known): ______

Do you have a budget? ☐ Yes ☐ No

Do you live within your means? ☐ Yes ☐ No ☐ Sometimes

Have you ever declared bankruptcy? ☐ Yes ☐ No

Any financial obligations not mentioned above? ___________________________

Areas of Concern:

Please check any areas where you have concerns or questions:

☐ Communication ☐ Conflict resolution ☐ Past relationships ☐ Sexual intimacy ☐ Finances
☐ In-laws/extended family ☐ Children/parenting ☐ Spiritual differences ☐ Personality differences
☐ Career/education ☐ Where to live ☐ Division of household tasks ☐ Addiction issues
☐ Past abuse/trauma ☐ Trust issues ☐ Other:

____

Brief Response Questions:

1. Why do you want to marry this person?

2. Do you have any fears or concerns about marriage? What are they?

3. What do you hope to gain from premarital counseling?

Signature: _________________________________ Date: __________

FORM 2: RELATIONSHIP HEALTH ASSESSMENT

For Advisor/Facilitator to complete after initial sessions

Couple Names: _________________________________ Date: _________

Rate each area on a scale of 1-5:

- 1 = Serious Concern (consider delaying wedding)
- 2 = Significant Issues (requires focused attention)
- 3 = Some Concerns (normal, addressable)
- 4 = Healthy (minor issues only)
- 5 = Excellent (strong foundation)

SPIRITUAL COMPATIBILITY

Both genuinely saved: ☐ Yes ☐ No ☐ Uncertain Rating: ☐ 1 ☐ 2 ☐ 3 ☐ 4 ☐ 5

Notes:

____

Similar spiritual maturity: ☐ Yes ☐ No ☐ Somewhat Rating: ☐ 1 ☐ 2 ☐ 3 ☐ 4 ☐ 5

Notes:

____

Agreement on essential doctrines: ☐ Yes ☐ No ☐ Mostly
Rating: ☐ 1 ☐ 2 ☐ 3 ☐ 4 ☐ 5

Notes:

____

Commitment to church involvement: ☐ Both ☐ One ☐ Neither
Rating: ☐ 1 ☐ 2 ☐ 3 ☐ 4 ☐ 5

Notes:

____

Plan for unified church attendance: ☐ Yes ☐ No ☐ Uncertain
Rating: ☐ 1 ☐ 2 ☐ 3 ☐ 4 ☐ 5

Notes:

____

Overall Spiritual Compatibility Rating: ☐ 1 ☐ 2 ☐ 3 ☐ 4 ☐ 5

RELATIONAL HEALTH

Quality of communication: Rating: ☐ 1 ☐ 2 ☐ 3 ☐ 4 ☐ 5

Notes:

Conflict resolution skills: Rating: ☐ 1 ☐ 2 ☐ 3 ☐ 4 ☐ 5

Notes:

Respect for each other: Rating: ☐ 1 ☐ 2 ☐ 3 ☐ 4 ☐ 5

Notes:

Trust level: Rating: ☐ 1 ☐ 2 ☐ 3 ☐ 4 ☐ 5

Notes:

Emotional intimacy: Rating: ☐ 1 ☐ 2 ☐ 3 ☐ 4 ☐ 5

Notes:

Evidence of unhealthy patterns (criticism, contempt, defensiveness, stonewalling):

☐ None ☐ Minimal ☐ Some ☐ Significant ☐ Severe Rating: ☐ 1 ☐ 2 ☐ 3 ☐ 4 ☐ 5

Specify:

Overall Relational Health Rating: ☐ 1 ☐ 2 ☐ 3 ☐ 4 ☐ 5

ROLES & EXPECTATIONS

Agreement on biblical roles: ☐ Yes ☐ No ☐ Somewhat Rating: ☐ 1 ☐ 2 ☐ 3 ☐ 4 ☐ 5

Notes:

Healthy understanding of headship/submission: ☐ Yes ☐ No ☐ Uncertain
Rating: ☐ 1 ☐ 2 ☐ 3 ☐ 4 ☐ 5

Notes:

Compatible expectations about careers: ☐ Yes ☐ No ☐ Uncertain
Rating: ☐ 1 ☐ 2 ☐ 3 ☐ 4 ☐ 5

Notes:

Agreement on children (if/when/how many): ☐ Yes ☐ No ☐ Uncertain
Rating: ☐ 1 ☐ 2 ☐ 3 ☐ 4 ☐ 5

Notes:

Compatible parenting philosophies: ☐ Yes ☐ No ☐ Uncertain ☐ N/A
Rating: ☐ 1 ☐ 2 ☐ 3 ☐ 4 ☐ 5

Notes:

Overall Roles & Expectations Rating: ☐ 1 ☐ 2 ☐ 3 ☐ 4 ☐ 5

FINANCIAL ALIGNMENT

Similar financial values: ☐ Yes ☐ No ☐ Somewhat Rating: ☐ 1 ☐ 2 ☐ 3 ☐ 4 ☐ 5

Notes:

____

Agreement on tithing: ☐ Both committed ☐ One committed ☐ Neither
Rating: ☐ 1 ☐ 2 ☐ 3 ☐ 4 ☐ 5

Notes:

____

Financial stability: ☐ Excellent ☐ Good ☐ Fair ☐ Poor
Rating: ☐ 1 ☐ 2 ☐ 3 ☐ 4 ☐ 5

Notes:

____

Debt management plan: ☐ Yes ☐ No ☐ N/A Rating: ☐ 1 ☐ 2 ☐ 3 ☐ 4 ☐ 5

Notes:

____

Financial transparency: ☐ Complete ☐ Partial ☐ Limited Rating: ☐ 1 ☐ 2 ☐ 3 ☐ 4 ☐ 5

Notes:

____

Overall Financial Alignment Rating: ☐ 1 ☐ 2 ☐ 3 ☐ 4 ☐ 5

FAMILY/BACKGROUND COMPATIBILITY

Similar family backgrounds: ☐ Yes ☐ No ☐ Somewhat Rating: ☐ 1 ☐ 2 ☐ 3 ☐ 4 ☐ 5

Notes:

____

Healthy extended family relationships: ☐ Both ☐ One ☐ Neither
Rating: ☐ 1 ☐ 2 ☐ 3 ☐ 4 ☐ 5

Notes:

____

Appropriate boundaries with families: ☐ Yes ☐ No ☐ Working on it
Rating: ☐ 1 ☐ 2 ☐ 3 ☐ 4 ☐ 5

Notes:

____

Previous marriage healing (if applicable): ☐ Yes ☐ No ☐ Partial ☐ N/A
Rating: ☐ 1 ☐ 2 ☐ 3 ☐ 4 ☐ 5

Notes:

____

Children's adjustment (if applicable): ☐ Good ☐ Fair ☐ Poor ☐ N/A
Rating: ☐ 1 ☐ 2 ☐ 3 ☐ 4 ☐ 5

Notes:

____

Overall Family/Background Compatibility Rating: ☐ 1 ☐ 2 ☐ 3 ☐ 4 ☐ 5

____

RED FLAG ASSESSMENT

Check any red flags present:

Critical Red Flags (Should Not Marry Without Resolution): ☐ One person not genuinely saved ☐ Active addiction (substance, pornography, gambling, etc.) ☐ Evidence of abuse (physical, emotional, verbal, spiritual) ☐ Active affair or recent infidelity during engagement ☐ Major deception/lies discovered ☐ Fundamental incompatibility on essential biblical issues ☐ Severe mental illness without treatment ☐ One person being coerced/pressured into marriage ☐ Legal issues (active warrants, serious charges pending)

Serious Red Flags (Require Significant Work): ☐ Significant spiritual immaturity (one or both) ☐ Major theological disagreements ☐ Unhealed wounds from past relationships/trauma ☐ Significant debt without disclosure or plan ☐ Patterns of destructive conflict ☐ Contempt or disrespect evident ☐ Children strongly opposed to marriage ☐ Toxic extended family without boundaries ☐ History of broken engagements ☐ Rushed timeline (known each other < 6 months)

Caution Flags (Need Attention): ☐ Communication needs improvement ☐ Some financial irresponsibility ☐ Minor theological differences ☐ Personality clashes requiring work ☐ One person significantly more mature ☐ Career/location uncertainties ☐ Sexual purity struggles during engagement ☐ Different expectations about important issues

---

OVERALL READINESS ASSESSMENT

Based on all factors, this couple's readiness for marriage is:

☐ **READY** - Strong foundation, minor issues only. Recommend proceeding with wedding as planned.

☐ **MOSTLY READY** - Generally healthy with some areas needing attention. Recommend completing all counseling and addressing identified issues before wedding.

☐ **NOT YET READY** - Significant issues present that need resolution. Recommend delaying wedding 3-6 months minimum while addressing concerns.

☐ **NOT COMPATIBLE** - Critical issues present that may indicate this couple should not marry. Recommend serious reconsideration of the relationship.

RECOMMENDATIONS:

What does this couple need to work on before marriage?

Are any referrals needed? (counseling, financial planning, etc.)

What specific action steps should they take?

Timeline recommendation:

☐ Proceed with wedding as planned ☐ Complete counseling, then reassess ☐ Delay wedding until specific issues resolved (specify timeline: ___________) ☐ Recommend canceling wedding

Additional notes:

Advisor Signature: _________________________________ Date: ___________

FORM 3: SESSION NOTES TEMPLATE

For Facilitator to complete after each session

Couple Names: ________________________________

Session #: ______ **Date:** ___________ **Duration:** ___________

Chapter/Topic Covered: _______________________________________

Attendance: ☐ Both present ☐ One absent (who: ___________)

Completion of Assignments:

☐ Both completed fully ☐ Both completed partially ☐ One didn't complete ☐ Neither completed

Notes:

____

KEY DISCUSSION POINTS:

1. ____
2. ____
3. ____

AREAS OF AGREEMENT:

AREAS OF DISAGREEMENT/CONCERN:

INSIGHTS GAINED:

About Him:

____

About Her:

____

About Their Relationship:

____

OBSERVATIONS:

Body language/interactions:

____

Concerning patterns:

____

Positive patterns:

____

ISSUES REQUIRING FOLLOW-UP:

    1. ____
    2. ____
    3. ____

ASSIGNMENTS FOR NEXT SESSION:

☐ Complete Chapter _______

☐ Other:

____

NEXT SESSION:

Date: ______________ Time: ______________ Location:

____

FACILTATOR'S PRIVATE NOTES:

(Impressions, concerns, prayer requests, etc.)

FORM 4: FINAL READINESS ASSESSMENT

To be completed after all counseling sessions

Couple Names: ____ Date: ____________

Counseling Period: From _____________ to _____________ (______ sessions)

Wedding Date: _____________

PROGRESS EVALUATION

Rate improvement in each area over the course of counseling:

Spiritual Growth: Beginning: ☐ 1 ☐ 2 ☐ 3 ☐ 4 ☐ 5 Ending: ☐ 1 ☐ 2 ☐ 3 ☐ 4 ☐ 5

Communication: Beginning: ☐ 1 ☐ 2 ☐ 3 ☐ 4 ☐ 5 Ending: ☐ 1 ☐ 2 ☐ 3 ☐ 4 ☐ 5

Conflict Resolution: Beginning: ☐ 1 ☐ 2 ☐ 3 ☐ 4 ☐ 5 Ending: ☐ 1 ☐ 2 ☐ 3 ☐ 4 ☐ 5

Understanding of Biblical Roles: Beginning: ☐ 1 ☐ 2 ☐ 3 ☐ 4 ☐ 5 Ending: ☐ 1 ☐ 2 ☐ 3 ☐ 4 ☐ 5

Financial Stewardship: Beginning: ☐ 1 ☐ 2 ☐ 3 ☐ 4 ☐ 5 Ending: ☐ 1 ☐ 2 ☐ 3 ☐ 4 ☐ 5

Overall Readiness: Beginning: ☐ 1 ☐ 2 ☐ 3 ☐ 4 ☐ 5 Ending: ☐ 1 ☐ 2 ☐ 3 ☐ 4 ☐ 5

STRENGTHS OF THIS COUPLE:

1. ____
2. ____
3. ____

AREAS STILL NEEDING GROWTH:

1. ____
2. ____
3. ____

UNRESOLVED ISSUES:

☐ None - all issues satisfactorily addressed

☐ Minor issues remain (specify):

____

☐ Significant issues remain (specify):

____

FINAL RECOMMENDATION:

☐ **READY TO MARRY** - This couple has completed counseling satisfactorily and demonstrated readiness for marriage. I recommend proceeding with the wedding and am willing to perform the ceremony.

☐ **READY WITH RESERVATIONS** - This couple has made progress but some concerns remain. I recommend they continue working on [specific areas] after marriage and am willing to perform the ceremony.

☐ **NOT READY** - Significant issues remain unresolved. I recommend delaying the wedding until [specific conditions met] and am not willing to perform the ceremony at this time.

☐ **SHOULD NOT MARRY** - Critical incompatibilities or issues present. I recommend this couple seriously reconsider marriage.

POST-MARRIAGE RECOMMENDATIONS:

☐ Continue in individual counseling (who: _______________) ☐ Continue in couples counseling ☐ Join married couples small group ☐ Attend marriage conference within first year ☐ Return for check-in at ______ months ☐ Read _________________________________ (book recommendation) ☐ Other:

____

CERTIFICATE

OF

COMPLETION

This certifies that _________________________________ and

____

have completed _______ sessions of premarital classes using the "Building on the Rock" workbook.

Date completed: _____________

☐ Certificate issued   ☐ Certificate withheld
(reason: ____)

Advisor/Facilitator's Signature:

____

Date: _____________

Title: ____

FORM 5: COUPLE FEEDBACK FORM

For couples to complete at end of the program.

Your Names: ____ Date: ____________

We value your feedback on the premarital class process. Please answer honestly:

1. How helpful was the "Building on the Rock" workbook overall?

☐ Extremely helpful ☐ Very helpful ☐ Somewhat helpful ☐ Not very helpful ☐ Not helpful

2. Which chapter was most helpful and why?

____

____

3. Which chapter was least helpful and why?

____

____

4. How would you rate your class facilitator?

☐ Excellent ☐ Very good ☐ Good ☐ Fair ☐ Poor

What did they do well?

____

____

What could they improve?

____

____

5. Did you feel comfortable being honest during sessions?

☐ Always ☐ Usually ☐ Sometimes ☐ Rarely ☐ Never

If not always, why?

____

6. What topics do you wish had been covered that weren't?

7. Do you feel better prepared for marriage after completing this material?

☐ Much better prepared ☐ Somewhat better prepared ☐ About the same ☐ Not better prepared

8. What was the most valuable thing you learned?

9. Would you recommend this facilitated class process to other engaged couples?

☐ Definitely ☐ Probably ☐ Maybe ☐ Probably not ☐ Definitely not

Why or why not?

10. Additional comments or suggestions:

Thank you for your feedback!